Great Expectations

D1574947

Cast and Creative Team

Joshua Asaré | Pip

Fresh out of training with the National Youth Theatre on their Playing Up course, Joshua's recent stage credits include *The Comedy Troll* at the Northwall Arts Centre and *THREE* at the Arcola Theatre.

Maryam Grace | Estella and Biddy

Maryam graduated from the Oxford School of Drama in 2015. Recent stage credits include Juliet in *Shit-Faced Shakespeare: Romeo and Juliet* and Shez in one woman show *Strawberry Starburst* at IYAF festival, for which she won the Best Individual Performance award. Her screen credits include *The Mummy* (2017).

Sarah Thom | Jo and Miss Havisham

Sarah trained with Jacques Lecoq in Paris. She works frequently on Radio 4, including playing the regular character, Joan, in the long-running comedy, *Clare in the Community*. In 2012, Sarah won the BBC Radio Drama Norman Beaton Fellowship. Sarah's extensive theatre work includes *Posh* (All Female – The Pleasance), *Bette and Joan: The Final Curtain* (St James Theatre, Assembly and UK tour), *A Taste of Honey* and *The Adventures of the Stoneheads* (National Theatre), *Mary Queen of Scots Got Her Head Chopped Off* (Kings Head), *Thatcher the Musical!* (UK tour), the role of Dido in *Dido Queen of Carthage* (Kensington Palace and the

House of St Barnabas-in-Soho) and most recently her own comedic play *Beak Speaks* at Underbelly. She co-founded site-specific Angels in the Architecture and from 2007–12 was Co-Artistic Director of Foursight Theatre. She is now a regular facilitator on the National Theatre's Theatreworks Programme. Television includes *Taboo, Not Going Out, Doctors* and *Stewart Lee's Comedy Vehicle* (BBC) and *Home Fires* (ITV).

Christopher Goh | Herbert Pocket and Compeyson

Christopher trained at the Actors Temple in 2011. Theatre credits include *The Arrest of Ai Wei Wei* (Hampstead Theatre), *Spill* (Southwark Playhouse) and *The 38th Parallel* (Park Theatre/ Arcola Theatre). Television credits include *Spooks, Doctors, Holby City* (BBC), *Coronation Street* (ITV), *Strikeback* (Cinemax), *The Five, You, Me and the Apocalypse* (Sky) and *The Royals* (E! Channel). Film credits include *Hunter Killer* (Millennium), *RPG* (MGN Filmes) and *The Power of the Heart* (NL BV films).

Liam Bewley | Magwycz and Mister Jaggers

Liam trained at Drama Centre London. Theatre credits include *Birthday Suit* (Old Red Lion – Nominated for an Offie Award for Best Actor), *Madame Manet* (Tabard Theatre), *Ace of Clubs* (The Union Theatre), *Margaret Catchpole* (Eastern Angles), *Three Faces of Evil* (New End Theatre) and *They Who Lay in the Field Like Beasts* (Theatre Royal Haymarket). Television includes *Silent Witness, Campus, Footballers' Wives, Extra Time* and *Celebdaq*. Film includes *The Double, The Waiting Room, The Diary of Tommy Crisp, Stand Up For Charlie Barr, Everywhere Is Nowhere, Luck, Channel Six, The Anchor* and *Macbeth*.

Peter Wicks | Orlick and Bentley Drummle

Peter was awarded the NSDF/RSC/Spotlight Emerging Artists Best Actor commendation for his role in *A Hero of Our Time* (Edinburgh Festival/Rose Theatre Kingston). Theatre credits include *The Alchemist* (Rose Playhouse), *The Elder Brother* (Globe Theatre) and, with Crowley & Co., *The Awkward Ghost* (VAULT Festival). Peter has also performed at the King's Head Theatre, the Drayton Arms, the Rose Theatre Kingston, Theatre503, the White Bear and the New Wimbledon Theatre.

Tom Crowley | Writer and Director

Tom is best known as a series writer and performer in the Prix Europa-nominated podcast sitcom *Wooden Overcoats* and as the playwright behind the stage adaptation of the *Rocky Horror* sequel, *Shock Treatment* (King's Head Theatre). He has also adapted a series of children's stories for the stage at Trinity Theatre, Tunbridge Wells, where he is an Associate Artist, and co-wrote the book for new musical *The Quentin Dentin Show* (Tristan Bates Theatre). Tom is the Artistic Director of theatre and events company Crowley & Co., with whom he has directed and produced *Radioman* (Old Red Lion Theatre), a two-week residency at VAULT Festival 2016 entitled *The Locker* and co-produced *Greywing House* by Molly Beth Morossa (Old Red Lion, VAULT Festival). With the company, Tom also produces and MCs *The Night*, a monthly variety showcase at Brasserie Zédel, and co-produces *Story Etc.*, a monthly fiction anthology podcast.

crowleynco.com | @crowleynco

Odinn Orn Hilmarsson | Composer and Sound Designer

Odinn is an Icelandic composer and filmmaker based in London. Since graduating with an MA in Digital Film and Television Production from the University of York, he has been working in theatre, film and podcasts making music, sound and various forms of video content. Recently Odinn has worked on several plays at

VAULT Festival 2017 including *Crocodile*, *Siren* and Casual Violence's *Grot in the Grotto*. In 2016 he was the composer for the comedy podcast *Hector Vs The Future* and worked on Crowley & Co.'s production of Felix Trench's *Radioman* at the Old Red Lion Theatre. Recently, Odinn has composed music for the National Youth Theatre's production of *Jekyll and Hyde*, which opened on the West End at the Ambassadors Theatre in October 2017.

Clancy Flynn | Set, Lighting and Costume Designer

Clancy is the lighting designer for the hugely popular ongoing touring production of *Trainspotting Live* and the technical designer for ImmerCity theatre company. They previously worked with Crowley & Co. as technical manager and lighting designer for their VAULT 2016 residency, *The Locker*. Clancy has also been a relighter or associate for other designers including Lee Curran, Malcolm Rippeth and Nic Farman. Design credits include *Paper Hearts* (Upstairs at the Gatehouse), *Piece of Silk* (Hope Theatre), *Portia* (Theatre503), *A Midsummer Night's Dream* (Pleasance), *Crocodile* (Network Theatre), *Chemsex Monologues* (King's Head Theatre) and *Little Red Riding Hood* (Gaiety Theatre and Swansea Grand).

Gina Abolins | Schools and Education Outreach

Gina has experience running programmes of educational and participatory work in theatre for the Ambassador Theatre Group and Out of Joint. She has coordinated and run workshops and courses for children and young people of all ages and is thrilled to be working with Crowley & Co. and the Heritage Arts Company on this brilliant, accessible modern adaptation of such a classic story.

Mat Burt | Line Producer

Mat Burt joined the Heritage Arts Company for their debut production *Where Soldiers Sleep* in 2008, and is their Creative Director. He is a producer, director and writer, and enjoys working with a wide variety of organisations throughout the UK, creating experiences for festivals, theatres, games and radio. He enjoys Tapirs and video games, both of which he tries to involve in his productions wherever possible. @batmurt

The Heritage Arts Company | Producer

The Heritage Arts Company (Mat Burt, Andy George and Tim Wilson) creates cultural events that excite the public imagination. Their guiding principles are equality and honesty, above everything else. As well as the annual VAULT Festival, London's biggest arts festival, they have so far created or produced radio plays, straight theatre, immersive events, gallery installations, multiplayer games and educational experiences, amongst others. They have worked with, or created work for, the Battersea Arts Centre, the National Theatre, Punchdrunk, Standon Calling, The Shunt Lounge, Secret Cinema, The British Fashion Council, Google, King's Cultural Institute, Lumin, Sky Atlantic, The Hospital Club, Old Vic Tunnels, IdeasTap, Kindle Theatre, Hammer Horror, The Roundhouse, English Heritage and more.

www.heritagearts.co.uk | @HeritageArts

The production would like to thank Anna Cook, John Martin and Alison Kemp of Trinity Theatre, Rishi Trikha, London Metropolitan University, VAULT Festival, Anton Rice, Dr Jen Sugden, Dr Jean Elliott, Tobias Wilson, Molly Beth Morossa and Gemma Arrowsmith for their support of the project.

A previous version of this adaptation of *Great Expectations* was produced by London Contemporary Theatre. It opened at the South Hill Park Arts Centre on 17 September 2014 and then toured the United Kingdom until 17 October 2014 with the following cast and creative team:

Jonathan Brindley | Pip
Catherine Thorncombe | Estella and Biddy
Lucy Peacock | Jo and Miss Havisham
Kaiden DuBois | Herbert Pocket and Compeyson
Joey Dexter | Magwycz and Mister Jaggers
Adam Tucker | Orlick and Bentley Drummle
Produced by Philip Ryder and Jonathan Ashby-Rock for London Contemporary Theatre
Directed by Jonathan Ashby-Rock
Associate Director: Lucy Grudniewicz
Music and Sound by Philip Ryder
Lighting Design by Jordan Lightfoot
Production Assistants: Ellie Muscutt and Amelia Butcher

Great Expectations for the Twenty-first Century

Great Expectations is perhaps one of Charles Dickens's best known and best loved novels. It was first published in weekly instalments from December 1860 to August 1861 in *All The Year Round*, a magazine which Dickens himself owned. The serialisation of novels in this way was common during the nineteenth century, and popular novelists like Dickens had the power to boost the circulation of a publication with their work. In fact, Dickens had originally planned to serialise *Great Expectations* monthly, but revised his plan (writing it in weekly parts instead) when it became apparent that his periodical could do with a boost in sales figures after Charles Lever's *A Day's Ride* proved unpopular with *All The Year Round*'s readership.

As Deborah Wynne has pointed out in *The Sensation Novel and the Victorian Family Magazine* (Houndmills: Palgrave, 2001), serialisation also presented authors with the opportunity to respond to important social and cultural debates of the day, debates which were simultaneously being discussed in other articles which appeared in a publication's pages alongside the serialised novel. *Great Expectations* is no exception, and in Pip's growth and development we see Dickens exploring a range of contemporary ideas and concerns, including: class, nature versus nurture, identity, education, and what makes a gentleman.

Dickens's rendering of his world is so rich with realistic detail, so evocative of Victorian England, that it is easy to overlook any relevance it might carry today. Setting his adaptation in the present day, Tom Crowley challenges his audience to think carefully about those social failings which reveal that some things have not changed all that much since Dickens put pen to paper. Class divides and equality of opportunity, for example, appear every bit as relevant now as they did back then, and the exploration is just as uncomfortable. Crowley's decision to recast Joe as Jo, a single working mother struggling to pay the rent in a run-down flat, plays a key role in highlighting this, as does the contrast drawn between Pip's background and Bentley Drummle's unearned privilege – just as striking here as it was in the original text.

At the heart of Crowley's play is an exploration of the self which echoes Dickens's own. Both texts are deeply interested in questions about our own self-knowledge; our moral fortitude; and how much control we have over our own destiny, the extent to which it is shaped by chance or others, and the impact this has on our own sense of self. In many respects *Great Expectations* offers a rather depressing take on human failings – not least our selfishness – which Crowley does not shy away from. That is not to say that the play does not have many moments of levity and genuine joy, yet in capturing the novel's bleaker aspects, and placing them in a modernised setting designed to remind us of the many social problems we face today, Crowley's play suggests that a bleak Dickensian lens might very well be a useful tool for understanding Britain in 2017.

*Dr Jen Sugden (Visiting University Lecturer
and Tutor in Nineteenth-century Literature), November 2017*

Great Expectations

Characters

Pip Pirrip, *aged 16, 20, 25 and 36. Young, scrappy, rough around the edges, has a temper. Ambitious without any idea of how to realise these ambitions. Later in life, he is transformed into a product of genteel city living, but is troubled by the sensation that he has lost sight of where he came from and what constitutes being a good person.*

Abel Magwycz, *aged 53 and 62. Born into poverty in Eastern Europe and raised as a mercenary killer, used to having to fight to survive. A ferocious exterior conceals the soul of a man who just wants to survive, and would love to be able to show kindness to someone, if only he were ever shown it himself.*

Jo Gargery, *aged 35, 39, 44 and 55. A female constable working for the Kent Police. Lost her daughter and her husband in a car accident many years ago, left with her son Pip. Unsophisticated and plain-spoken, but smart and very resilient of spirit. A devoted and caring mother, despite her short fuse.*

Compeyson, *aged 49 and 58. Of upper-class birth, underhanded, scheming and a dirty fighter. Has seen both military service with the British Army and private mercenary work with the Brentford Security Company.*

Orlick, *aged 22, 26 and 31. A brutish, brash police constable, Jo's colleague in the Kent Police. A leering presence in the house, he tries to ingratiate himself as a father figure to Pip in order to try to find his way into Jo's bed. Also a fiend for the drink, with a habit of over-indulging and speaking out of turn.*

Biddy, *aged 17, 21 and 26. Modest, thoughtful and honest. Pip's oldest schoolfriend, studious and considerate. An orphan, living with her uncaring great aunt. By escaping to Pip and Jo's flat as often as she can, she has found a second home there.*

Estella, *aged 16, 25 and 36. Raised to be beautiful, elegant and completely heartless. Since birth, she has been raised by Miss Havisham as an instrument of revenge, rather than as a person. As she gets older, she becomes resentful of her guardian and has adopted* *a guarded manner of self-preservation, unable to love or trust any other living being.*

Miss Havisham, *aged 52, 56 and 61. Lives in stately Satis House with her ward, Estella, still wearing the wedding dress she was stood up in. She is proud, vain, embittered and fixated with punishing men for the hurt that was done to her. She is distrustful of anybody who shows her kindness, as she assumes they are after her money. As such, she has shunned all of her former friends and all of her living relatives.*

Herbert Pocket, *aged 20, 24 and 29. Kind and intelligent, but a touch reckless. Prone to over-indulging in drink and revelry. A Junior Research Fellow in the Law department of LSE and Pip's closest friend and confidant in London. Wants to strike out into private practice but can't keep hold of money long enough to gather the start-up collateral.*

Mister Jaggers, *aged 44 and 49. Forceful and intimidating, but beneath it all, a good and reliable person. Has a history of dealing with unruly clients as a private solicitor, and more recently of dealing with unruly students as a Lecturer in Law at LSE.*

Bentley Drummle, *aged 24–29. From old money. A Law student at LSE a few years ahead of Pip. He and Pip quickly establish a peaceful mutual disdain. Rich, good-looking and smug. Nicknamed the Spider for his habit of hanging on the edge of parties, waiting to the right opportunity to pounce on unsuspecting young ladies.*

Casting note: the text is written to allow for double casting as follows: **Magwycz** *is doubled with* **Jaggers**, **Jo** *with* **Miss Havisham**, **Biddy** *with* **Estella**, **Herbert** *with* **Compeyson** *and* **Orlick** *with* **Drummle**.

One

Pip *stands and addresses the audience.*

Pip My father's family name being Pirrip, and my first name being Philip, as a little boy I couldn't make anything clearer out of either name than 'Pip'. So I called myself 'Pip', and came to be called 'Pip'.

Pip *continues, now addressing the ground in front of him – the graves of his father and sister in the churchyard. He is 16. He speaks in the way that people do when they think nobody can hear them.*

I don't know what else to be. I'm not Philip, that's for sure. You were Alexandra, but not for very long. You might've been Alexandra, or Alex, or Sandra. Whatever you wanted. S'pose we'll never know.

Pip *looks at the grave beside.*

Our dad was Philip, yeah. Definitely Philip. That's a strong name. A dad's name. If he were still here, I could have left all the Philip stuff to him. Or maybe he'd have made sure I did my time when he got sick of it. Can't hardly remember Dad.

Pip *looks back to Alexandra's grave.*

And you, we haven't even got a single clue what you were gonna look like when you grew up. Maybe the way they've written your name in the stone? That's all we've got to go on. How rubbish is that?

Pip *inspects the words, 'Alexandra Pirrip'.*

I'm thinking . . . freckles? Would we have had room, if we'd lost Dad but not you? Room for Alexandra? Another mouth to feed, just another kid taking up space, probably.

But it might have done Mum some good to have a little Sandra to talk to, about things Pips don't understand.

Pip *lays a hand on his sister's grave.*

Magwycz *appears behind him, in handcuffs. Before* **Pip** *notices him,* **Magwycz** *has grabbed* **Pip** *and holds him in a headlock.*

Magwycz   Hold your noise! Keep still, little devil, or I cut your throat!

Pip   Don't, please! Please!

Magwycz   Your name? Quick!

Pip   Pip!

Magwycz   Again, give it mouth.

Pip   Pip. It's Pip.

Magwycz   Pip. I hear you talking. Who you were talking to?

Pip   Her!

Pip *points at the ground.* **Magwycz** *jumps, then understands. He reads the tombstone.*

Magwycz   Alexandra Pirrip. 1994–1995. Hm! Just one year. Still, one year is not easy to live, for a little thing least of all. You want to live one more year, you listen and you do what I say. This your sister, this your father, yes?

Pip   Yes.

Magwycz *gently pulls* **Pip** *backwards, so he is forced to bend back, off-balance.*

Magwycz   Your mother is alive, at least?

Pip   Yes.

Magwycz   Who is she?

Pip   Jo Gargery. She's . . . she's a police officer.

Magwycz   Jo Gargery. Police. Is good. Is very good. You know where is keys?

Pip   Keys?

Magwycz   For handcuffs, all police have keys for handcuffs!

Pip   Yes! Yes, I know.

Magwycz   Good.

Magwycz *lifts* **Pip** *back up to a standing position, then takes the handcuffs away from his throat.*

Magwycz   You will take me to a place I can sleep for few days. Here, near the marshes, is very cold at night. I get wet, I get sick, I get dead. No good.

Pip   I don't know . . . wait. There's a whole floor in our building nobody lives in, burnt out. It's been empty for years, they haven't even fixed it up since. No one goes in there.

Magwycz   Good. You take me there, and then you give me keys.

Magwycz *grabs* **Pip** *by the arm, firmly.*

Magwycz   Also you bring me food, and drink, and you don't tell anybody you see me, or else I take out your heart and liver. Then I cut off your fat little boy cheeks, and I eat them.

Pip   Yes. Yes.

Magwycz   And that is least trouble. I am not alone, though you may think so. There is a young man hid with me, and compared with him, I am an angel. This young man, he have ways of getting to a young boy's heart, and liver, and if a boy hide from him, he hide in vain. The boy may lock his door, may be warm in bed, may tuck himself up, but this young man, he find his way to this boy, and he will tear him open.

At this moment, I am stopping young man from harming you, with very much difficulty. Very hard for me to keep this young man away from your insides. Now what do you say?

Trying not to let his voice waver, **Pip** *points towards home with his free hand.*

Pip   This way.

Magwycz *lets him go.* **Pip** *leaves in the direction of home with* **Magwycz** *close behind.* **Magwycz** *looks all around him as they go, terrified of detection.*

Magwycz   Good boy.

Two

Jo*'s flat, later that night.* **Pip** *sneaks in, looking furtive. He takes stock of the environs, looking around for any sign of* **Jo***'s keys.*

Enter **Jo***, still in her uniform, unseen by* **Pip***. She shouts and gives* **Pip** *a start.*

Jo   Where have you been?!

Pip   Nowhere!

Jo   Pip, it's late, I've been looking for you!

Jo *grabs for* **Pip** *and he runs across the room.*

Pip   I'm sorry!

Jo   Down at the school, and all over the building, and everywhere in between!

Pip   I'm fine!

Jo   What if you hadn't been? What if you got yourself hurt and you ended up lying in a gutter somewhere and nobody knew where you were?!

Pip   Mum, nothing happened, I'm fine!

Jo   So where have you been all this time?!

Pip   I was at the churchyard!

Jo *stops in her tracks.* **Pip** *is shaky, frightened, trying not to cry.*

Pip   I was at the churchyard. I was just visiting Dad and Alexandra, Mum, that's all it was. I just wanted to go see them. That's all.

Jo   Oh, Pip, no.

Jo *reaches a hand out to* **Pip***. He flinches.*

Jo   Pip, no, please, I'm sorry.

Jo *throws her arms around* **Pip**.

Pip   Mum, it's okay.

Jo   I just get so frightened.

Pip   I know, Mum, I know.

Jo   I have to watch those children getting themselves hurt or killed or worse, all day.

Pip   Mum.

Jo   What if one day that's you?

Pip   It won't be, I promise, Mum.

Jo *releases* **Pip** *from her embrace, rubs her eyes. She puts her keys down on the table – the handcuff key as well as front door, car keys, etc.* **Pip** *spots them.*

Jo   I'm tired. That's all.

Pip   Yes, Mum.

Jo   Another long day.

Pip   I'm sorry, Mum.

Jo   No, don't be sorry.

Jo *hugs* **Pip** *again.*

Jo   It's not your fault.

Jo *lets go of* **Pip** *and walks out, taking off her jacket as she goes.*

Jo   Don't forget to turn off the kitchen light before you go to bed.

Pip   No, Mum, I won't.

Pip *watches* **Jo** *go to bed, then, when she is safely away, he takes her keys off the table and stuffs them in his pocket. He leaves to gather the other supplies for* **Magwycz** *– stopping short only to turn the kitchen light off as he goes.*

Three

Pip *sneaks through the empty floor of his flat block, carrying a shopping bag.*

There is a figure in a large overcoat lurking in the corner, which **Pip** *assumes to be* **Magwycz**. *It is, in fact,* **Compeyson**.

Pip   Hello? I brought the –

Compeyson *starts and turns around. He is also wearing handcuffs. He sees* **Pip** *and flees.* **Pip** *is startled, but stands fast.*

Pip   Hello? Are you there?

Magwycz *appears behind* **Pip**. *He makes* **Pip** *jump.*

Magwycz   Not so loud, boy. You bring keys? Food?

Pip *silently holds out his offerings.* **Magwycz** *grabs the shopping bag and the keys.*

Magwycz   Is which keys?

Pip   I don't know.

Magwycz *grunts in irritation. He sits down and takes the food and drink out of the bag. He is happy to find a pork pie in the bag, much happier to find a bottle of brandy. He takes a big bite of the pie, a big swig of the brandy and sets to work trying each key in the handcuffs.*

Magwycz   Not best brandy, but good.

An awkward silence as **Magwycz** *fiddles with the keys.* **Pip** *mutters.*

Pip   I'm glad you like it.

Magwycz   What, boy? You speak?

Pip   I said I'm glad you like it.

Magwycz   Thank you, boy. I do.

Magwycz *eventually finds the right key and casts away the handcuffs. He throws the ring of keys back to* **Pip** *with a laugh of triumph. He takes another big swig from the bottle.*

Pip   Aren't you saving any for the young man?

Magwycz *looks up in a panic.*

Magwycz Young man? Oh. No, he don't drink. He don't need food tonight, neither.

Pip He looked like he did.

Magwycz *looks at* **Pip** *with suspicion.*

Magwycz You seen him? Where?

Pip Just over by the lifts. I think I scared him, he went right off down the emergency stairs.

Magwycz Right. Yes. Must be him. Young man. What did he look like?

Pip He was dressed similar to you, in a big coat. Plus, he. . .

Magwycz What? He what?

Pip He had the same reason for needing keys.

Magwycz Yes. Good.

Magwycz *looks very distressed but tries to conceal it.*

Emergency stairs?

Pip Yeah, just that way.

Pip *indicates the direction in which* **Compeyson** *fled.*

Magwycz Thank you, boy.

Magwycz *gathers up the remaining brandy and food into the shopping bag and sprints off towards the stairs.*

Pip Wait, won't he need the . . .?

Pip *holds up the keys, confused. He steps back, warily, then runs back the way he came in.*

Four

Jo's *flat, the following evening.* **Jo**, *currently 35, fusses around, setting the table.* **Orlick**, *22, still in police uniform, sits at the* *dinner table, already tipsy, swigging from a bottle of beer. He guffaws obnoxiously, more amused by his own stories than* **Jo** *is.*

Orlick   So these girls have no time for Martin whatsoever, not interested, so Martin, he's getting a bit rowdy, and he says to this one, 'I'll kill you!' I was pissing myself already, but then Tony grabs Martin by the scruff of the neck and flings him into a hedgerow! Took him a good six minutes to scrabble his way out!

As **Orlick** *laughs his way through this story,* **Pip** *enters with* **Biddy**, *17.*

Jo   Bloody lovely, Orlick, an example to the community as usual – Oh, hello Biddy. How was the maths mock?

Pip   That was yesterday.

Biddy   It was fine, Miz Gargery, thank you.

Orlick   Pair of geniuses, the both of you. Of course, old Pip over here, I taught him everything he knows.

Biddy *quietly and politely sits down at the table.*

Jo   Yes, Orlick.

Orlick   Look at you now, just fifteen and already a big strapping lad.

Pip   Sixteen.

Orlick   Stands to reason, you needed a strong man around the house, and lucky for you, old Orlick was here to provide.

Jo   Biddy, do you want some dinner? There's enough for three.

Orlick   Proof is in the pudding.

Biddy   No, Miz Gargery, it's fine, I'm sure Auntie will have something for me at home.

Pip   She didn't last night.

Biddy   Pip!

Orlick   Of course, that's what a young girl wants, a strong man, isn't that right, Biddy?

Jo   Oh, nonsense, Biddy, Auntie can keep, I'll put some extra on for you.

Orlick   Isn't it, Biddy?

Biddy   Pardon, Mister Orlick?

Orlick   You'll be scouting about for a nice young man or three, pretty girl of your age.

Jo   Orlick.

Orlick   Lucky there's plenty of it about, eh, Pip?

Jo   ORLICK.

Orlick   What, I'm just –

Jo   I'll see you tomorrow.

There is a very awkward pause. **Pip** *and* **Biddy** *try their best not to look at each other or at* **Orlick**. **Jo** *stares* **Orlick** *down.*

Orlick   Well, time I made a move. Nice to see you kids, Constable Gargery, I'll see you at the station. Supposed to be a cold night. Better bundle up warm.

Orlick *looks* **Jo** *up and down. He nods a last goodbye, then exits.*

Jo   Sorry about that, kids.

Biddy   It's alright, Miz Gargery.

Pip   Just Orlick.

Jo   Anyway. Never mind that. Dinner. Fish fingers alright for you, Biddy?

Biddy   Lovely, Miz Gargery.

Offstage a phone rings. **Jo** *exits to answer it.*

Biddy   Nice of your Mum.

Pip   I hate how he looks at her.

Biddy   I'm sure he doesn't mean anything by it.

Pip   I'm sure he does.

Biddy   Jo can take care of herself.

Pip   Yeah.

Biddy *looks at* **Pip**, *unsure what to say.*

Jo *comes back in, putting on her police jacket.*

Jo   Change of plan, I'm afraid, Biddy, dinner will have to wait.

Pip   What's happened?

Jo   Couple of men escaped custody a week ago, apparently they've been spotted in the area.

Pip *is stunned into silence, he feels a cold chill run through him.*

Biddy   What men? Are they dangerous?

Jo   Dangerous enough that you're coming with me.

Pip   What?

Jo   I'm not having you kids home alone, they might get into the building. Get your coats. I'll take you home once we've done a sweep of the area, Biddy.

Pip   Mum, it's fine, we'll just lock ourselves in.

Jo   I wouldn't expect that door to stand up against a stiff breeze. And if someone comes in here and tears your head off, I won't be the one stitching it back on again, believe you me. You're coming.

Biddy   Where were they seen, Miz Gargery?

Jo   Near the churchyard. Keep your eyes peeled and don't run off.

Biddy *follows* **Jo** *out.* **Pip** *lingers, looking terrified.*

Jo   Pip! Now!

Pip *runs after them.*

Five

Jo *enters sweeping a torch around the dimly-lit stage.* **Pip** *and* **Biddy** *follow close behind as she searches the churchyard.*

Biddy You alright?

Pip I'm fine, it's just cold.

Biddy You're not scared.

Pip No.

Biddy I am. I think you're crazy not to be.

Pip I hope we don't find them.

Jo I'll give you twenty quid if they've cut and run already. They'll be lying low.

Biddy They did say the churchya –

Biddy *is cut off by* **Magwycz** *and* **Compeyson**, *who launch onto stage together, locked in a life-or-death struggle.* **Compeyson** *still wears handcuffs.* **Compeyson** *screams and flails,* **Magwycz** *laughs maniacally, tearing into* **Compeyson**. **Jo** *waves* **Biddy** *and* **Pip** *away, points her torch at the two wanted men.*

Compeyson Please! Please!

Jo You two! Stop right there, Police!

Compeyson *scrabbles over to* **Jo**, *his hands up.* **Magwycz** *stands, cackling.* **Pip** *and* **Biddy** *cower, further back.* **Pip** *tries to avoid* **Magwycz**'s *gaze.* **Jo** *speaks into her walkie-talkie.*

Jo Come in, dispatch, this is four-five-zero, request immediate backup at the churchyard.

Magwycz I took him! Remember this! I bring him to you!

Jo I'm not interested, I'm afraid, sir, I need you to lie face down on the ground –

Magwycz I don't need it to do good for me. He knows I took him. That is enough.

Compeyson, *severely beaten, distances himself from* **Magwycz**, *pleads with* **Jo**.

Compeyson   Stop him! He's trying to kill me!

Magwycz   If I try to kill you, you be already dead! No, I take this man and I bring him to you, so this gentleman villain faces justice! You take me too, I don't care, I could have get away if I wanted, but no.

Jo   Face down on the ground, hands on your head.

Compeyson   He tried to kill me, I'm telling you!

Magwycz   Look at this liar's eyes! Just like in the van, he will not look at me!

Compeyson   You're not much to look at anyway!

Jo   ON THE GROUND!

Compeyson *surrenders, lies down as instructed.* **Jo** *looks to* **Magwycz**. *Smiling a wicked smile, he lies down too.* **Jo** *handcuffs* **Magwycz**.

Enter **Orlick**, *still slightly drunk.*

Jo   And where the hell have you been?

Orlick   I came as quick as I could.

Jo *stands* **Magwycz** *up.* **Orlick** *helps* **Compeyson** *to his feet.* **Compeyson** *stands facing away from* **Magwycz**. **Pip** *and* **Biddy** *still cower in the distance.* **Magwycz** *sees* **Pip**, *stares at him.*

Jo   As quick as you can when you're half-cut, you mean.

Orlick   I'm here now, aren't I?

Magwycz *calls to* **Jo**, *still staring at* **Pip**.

Magwycz   Madam Constable?

Pip *tries without much luck to conceal his utter panic.*

Jo   Just Constable, thank you.

Magwycz   This is your son?

Pip *is terrified, certain that he is about to be given up.*

Jo   What business is that of yours? Pip, just stay back.

Magwycz   Pip. You look like nice boy. Your mother raise you well.

Jo   Don't you speak to him. Just get moving. Orlick?

Orlick   Yes, Jo. Come on, you.

Jo *and* **Orlick** *drag* **Magwycz** *and* **Compeyson** *offstage.*

Compeyson   He's crazy, I tell you, he wants me dead!

Orlick   Shut up and get in the van.

The police and the convicts are gone. **Pip** *heaves a sigh of relief.*

Biddy   I knew you were scared.

Pip   Wasn't.

Biddy   You looked like you were about to wee yourself.

Pip   Maybe a little bit.

Biddy   Not surprised. That big one, the way he looked at you.

Pause.

Exciting though. Better than telly.

Pip   I'd better take you home, your aunt will be getting worried.

Biddy   Long as you're okay.

Pip   I'll live.

Pip's *'I'll live' sends us forward in time.* **Biddy** *leaves.*

Six

A few months later. **Pip** *lurks around in the street outside Satis House. He looks uncomfortable.* **Orlick** *appears, gazing up at the stately home.*

Orlick   Just look at the place.

Pip   What am I doing here?

Orlick   'Satis House'.

Pip *mishears this as 'Is that his house?'*

Pip   Is that whose house?

Orlick   No, 'Satis House', look. It's the name. It's Miss Havisham owns it.

Pip   What does she want?

Orlick   Be civil, mate, there might be something in this for you.

Pip   Like what?

Orlick   Jo and me got talking to Miss Havisham last week, we got called on a false alarm, mad old bat thought there was somebody trying to get in. Anyway, she told us she's got a girl living with her about your age who needs a bit of company.

Pip   Do I have to?

Orlick   Come on, Pip, pretty girl with a bit of money in her pocket.

Pip   Shut up.

Orlick   Oi, behave. Your mum said you'd pay a visit, so you're paying a visit. Where's the doorbell on this –

Estella *appears from inside, surprising* **Orlick**.

Orlick   Oh! Good afternoon, miss.

Estella   What do you want?

Orlick   We're here to see Miss Havisham.

Estella   She doesn't want to see you.

Orlick   Ha, um, I believe she does, young lady. She asked me to bring this young gentleman here to visit.

Estella *looks at* **Pip**. *He squirms under scrutiny.*

Estella   So this is the boy.

Orlick   Yes, this is Miz Gargery's –

Estella   You can come in.

Pip   Alright.

Estella   You go away.

Orlick   Well, nice to –

Estella *turns her back on* **Orlick** *and disappears back into the house.*

Orlick   Good bloody luck.

Orlick *walks away. After steeling himself for a moment,* **Pip** *follows* **Estella** *in.*

Pip *and* **Estella** *reappear, now inside Satis House. They stop and look around the yard, awkwardly silent.*

Estella   The old brewery.

Pip   Oh. Yeah, I see.

Estella   You could easily drink all the beer that's brewed there now, boy.

Pip   Thanks?

Estella   Do you know what Satis House means, boy?

Pip   No. When the man who dropped me off said 'Satis House', I thought he meant, uh . . . I thought . . .

Estella's *glare silences* **Pip**.

Pip   No.

Estella   It's Latin. It means 'Enough'.

Pip   Enough house?

Estella   Whoever built it wanted to imply that whatever person owned this house could want for nothing more. They must have been curiously easily pleased in those days.

Pip   I don't think it's so –

Estella *laughs at* **Pip***'s pronunciation of 'think' as 'fink'.*

Estella   Do you really speak like that? All the time?

Pip   What?

Estella   'I fort', 'I fink'. How does one get through life sounding like that?

Pip *is shocked, stuck for words.*

Estella   What, boy? Nothing to say in your defence?

Pip   If you don't like how I talk, I won't.

Estella *scoffs.*

Estella   Alright, 'Fink', suit yourself. Here.

They are now at an extreme end of the stage. **Estella** *indicates the opposite end of the stage, another room.*

Go in.

Pip *starts to obey, then catches himself and stops.*

Pip   Uh, after you.

Estella   Don't be ridiculous, Fink, I'm not going in.

Pip *nods and walks in. From offstage,* **Miss Havisham***'s voice can be heard.*

Miss Havisham   Who's there?

Pip   Fi – Pip, Miss.

Miss Havisham   Pip?

Pip   Constable Gargery's son, Miss, come to visit.

Enter **Miss Havisham**. *Worn, tired, half-blind, but elegant and almost seeming to glide under the pleats of her old, weather-beaten wedding dress.*

Miss Havisham   Come closer. Let me look at you.

Pip *cautiously steps nearer to* **Miss Havisham**.

Miss Havisham   Are you frightened by the sight of somebody who hasn't seen the sun since before you were born?

Pip *thinks carefully about the answer he is supposed to give.*

Pip   No?

Miss Havisham *looks at* **Pip** *and smiles unpleasantly.*

Miss Havisham   Look.

Miss Havisham *puts her hands over her heart.*

What do you suppose is here?

Pip   Your heart.

Miss Havisham   Broken. Broken long ago.

I sometimes have sick fancies. I fancy now that I should like to see someone play.

Play.

Pip   I don't . . . I don't know what I should play, Miss.

Miss Havisham   Very well. Call Estella. Call her at the door. You can do that, boy.

Pip, *halting, very unsure of himself, goes to where he walked in from.*

Pip   Estella? Estella!

Estella *appears, hugely irritated.*

Estella   Don't you call at me like I'm a maid, Fink.

Miss Havisham *produces a deck of cards, seemingly from nowhere.*

Miss Havisham   I told young Pip to call for you, Estella. I would like you to play cards with him.

Estella   With him? But he's so . . . dull! Such a stupid, ignorant little boy.

Pip *looks away, flushing with anger and embarrassment.* **Miss Havisham** *beckons* **Estella** *over and whispers into her ear. Her words are barely audible.*

Miss Havisham   . . . you can break his heart . . .

Estella *rolls her eyes and turns to* **Pip***.*

Estella   Well? What do you play?

Pip   I can play poker.

Estella   That's ridiculous, we can't play poker without something to bet.

Pip   When my Mum and I play, we bet with matches.

Estella *looks at* **Pip** *with total disdain.* **Miss Havisham** *smiles, amused.*

Miss Havisham   Well, Estella? You can find the matches in the pantry.

Estella   Unbelievable.

Miss Havisham   Estella.

Estella *walks out to the pantry.* **Pip** *stands awkwardly in silence with* **Miss Havisham** *for a minute.*

Miss Havisham   What do you think of her?

Pip   Of Estella?

Miss Havisham   Yes.

Pip   I think she's very proud.

Miss Havisham   Anything else?

Pip   I think she's very pretty.

Miss Havisham   Anything else?

Pip   I think she's very insulting.

Miss Havisham   Anything else?

Pip   I think I want to go home.

Miss Havisham   And never see her again?

Pip   . . . I didn't say that.

Estella *reappears with a box of matches.*

Estella   We're almost out.

Miss Havisham   Never mind, Estella, young Pip is leaving us for the day.

Estella   Unbelievable!

Miss Havisham   Show him out.

Estella   Come on, Fink.

Miss Havisham   Wait a moment.

Miss Havisham *comes closer to* **Pip**, *and inspects him uncomfortably close-up.*

Miss Havisham   When will we have you back?

Pip   It's . . . it's Wednesday now, so –

Miss Havisham   No, no, NO! I know nothing of the days of the week, or the months of the year. Come back in six days. Now leave me.

Miss Havisham *leaves.* **Estella** *begins to follow, but* **Miss Havisham** *snaps at her.*

Miss Havisham   Both of you.

Pip *is shaken, completely humiliated, close to tears, but he hurriedly composes himself when* **Estella** *returns. She leans in to him, mimicking* **Miss Havisham**'s *inspection of him.* **Pip** *shrinks away from her.* **Estella** *laughs.*

Estella   Why don't you cry?

Pip   I don't want to cry.

Estella   Liar. You were just crying now. Your eyes are red. And you're not finished. You'll cry again soon, and you'll cry until you are half-blind. So why don't you just cry?

Pip *stares into her eyes.*

Estella *chuckles and skips back into the house.* **Pip** *sniffles in frustrated anger, wipes his eyes and storms off.*

Seven

Jo'*s flat, that evening. Offstage, a toilet flushes.* **Orlick** *swaggers in drunkenly, holding a mostly-full bottle of beer. He greedily swills it down, finishes the bottle, then shakily sits down, very nearly missing the chair. He is too far gone and slurs his words. His reactions are sluggish and graceless.*

Enter **Pip**.

Orlick   Hey! How did it go, come on.

Pip   Fine.

Enter **Jo**.

Jo   Is that Pip? What happened?

Pip   You could have warned me.

Jo   She is a bit of an eccentric.

Orlick   Too right, daft old cow.

Jo   Orlick.

Pip   Did you know about the wedding dress thing?

Orlick   What happened, mate? How was that girl?

Jo   Yes, Estella, what was she like?

The mention of **Estella** *cuts* **Pip** *deeply, he is becoming frustrated at the line of questioning.*

Pip I don't want to talk about it.

Jo Well, you've got to give us something!

Orlick Was there anybody else in there?

Pip*, infuriated, decides he has to give them something.*

Pip Four dogs.

Jo Dogs? She's got dogs in that place?

Orlick What sort of dogs?

Pip Huge. Massive dogs. They ate big bits of raw meat out of a silver dish.

Jo Bloody hell.

Orlick Wouldn't put it past 'em. Toffs.

Jo Did you get to spend some time with Estella?

Pip Mum.

Jo Well, come on!

Pip *is losing all pretence of making things up. The more they believe him, the more irritated he becomes.*

Pip Yes, it was brilliant, we played with . . . flags.

Orlick *chuckles drunkenly.*

Orlick Oh, is that what you kids are calling it –

Jo Oi.

Pip Then we all had a big sword fight on the roof.

Orlick What, really?

Jo Where did you get swords from?

Pip They were stuck up on the wall, crossed, like in films.

Orlick   Mate, you want to sort your act out.

Pip   What?

Orlick   Well, it's pathetic, son. You're invited into some rich girl's house and all you do is play with swords like a five-year-old when you ought to be making nice.

Jo   Orlick, give it a rest.

Orlick   Look, I'm only saying.

Jo   Orlick, not all boys have to go chasing after every bit of skirt that comes their way.

Orlick   You're hurting my feelings, Jo, you're cutting me to the quick over here.

Jo   Don't try to tell my son how to be a man.

Orlick   Who else is going to do it? You? As if you know anything about courting, anyway.

Jo   Orlick.

Orlick   You won't give anybody the time of day.

Jo   Orlick, get out.

Orlick   No matter how nice they ask.

Jo   Just GET OUT!

Orlick *looks proudly at* **Jo**, *who scowls at him, and* **Pip**, *who looks away. He chuckles another seedy chuckle and goes to stagger out.*

Orlick   Better take myself to bed. It's not like anybody else is going to.

Exit **Orlick**, *weaving.*

Jo *goes to comfort* **Pip**.

Jo   What's the matter, Pip?

Pip   Nothing.

Jo   Well, first you won't talk, then you come out with a lot of gibberish about flags. Did something go wrong?

Pip It was embarrassing.

Jo But why?

Pip I'm ignorant.

Jo Oh, that's nonsense. You're on track for a B in Maths, Mister Wopsle said so. Though I'm sure that's something to do with Biddy's influence as well.

Pip I wish my voice didn't sound so stupid.

Jo Your voice doesn't –

Pip I wish I had a nice haircut and an expensive shirt. Fancy shoes. I wish I had an answer for everything. I wish I wasn't me.

Jo *considers* **Pip**. *She knows she can't give him all the things he wants. She stiffens.*

Jo Well, you sulk over the things you haven't got if you want, but if you ask me, you're better off being Pip.

Pip Mm.

Jo If you don't want to go back to see Miss Havisham again, you don't have to. But if you really want to pick up some fancy habits . . . no better way to get refined than mixing with refined people. You might learn something.

Jo *leaves, saddened.* **Pip** *thinks.* **Estella** *is all he can think about.*

Pip Well, maybe . . . maybe once more.

Estella *appears from nowhere.*

Estella You again, Fink.

Eight

Estella's *line has transported* **Pip** *from* **Jo**'s *flat back to Satis House, the next week.*

Pip Yes.

Estella   Unbelievable.

Estella *turns and flounces past* **Pip**, *leading them both into a montage of moments of* **Pip**'s *regular visits to Satis House.*

Estella *is positioned in the centre of the stage, while* **Pip** *orbits around her, his eyes fixed on her. He is drawn to her, but too afraid to approach, and so continues a silent orbit.* **Estella** *never looks at him, not even when she is addressing him. He is not there with her, but rather is observing as if in his own memory. Each of* **Estella**'s *lines is a snapshot from a different visit.*

Estella   Why do you keep bringing him here? We have nothing to talk about.

Eurgh, boy, do you never clean out your fingernails? You look like you've been digging in the compost pile.

Why don't you cry again, Fink?

For God's sake, that sound he makes when he eats! Don't let him have dinner here again, I'll be sick!

A new moment from a later visit. By this point **Miss Havisham** *has appeared and gleefully watches* **Pip** *and* **Estella**'s *dance.*

Estella   Do you still find me pretty?

A new moment from a later visit. **Miss Havisham** *walks to the centre and strokes* **Estella**'s *hair briefly as the montage of* **Estella**'s *lines continues.*

Estella   It's 'none of them IS', not 'none of them ARE', you idiot, have you never read a book?

A new moment from a later visit. **Miss Havisham** *leaves* **Estella** *and exits.*

Estella   Do you still find me insulting?

Finally, after months of visits, the montage ends. **Pip** *and* **Estella** *return to their positions from the beginning of the scene, with* **Pip** *waiting to be let into Satis House. Finally,* **Estella** *looks at him and addresses him directly.*

Estella   You again, Fink.

Pip   Yes.

Estella   Unbelievable.

Pip *joins* **Estella**, *who leads him into Satis House.*

Pip   Where's Miss Havisham?

There is a prolonged shriek of rage from offstage. It is **Miss Havisham**.

Estella   She's around.

Pip   What's the matter?

Estella   It's her birthday.

Miss Havisham *storms onto stage clutching a birthday card, waving it about in fury.*

Miss Havisham   Liars! Vultures! Traitors, all of them!

Pip   Uh. Happy bi –

Estella *slaps* **Pip** *in the face to stop him finishing the sentence.* **Pip** *is stunned.*

Miss Havisham   Listen to this! 'Many happy returns, old friend, it has been such a terribly long time since we saw one another. Hopefully next year Matthew and I will be allowed to visit you on your birthday in person –' HA! Sarah and Matthew Pocket! They'll visit just long enough to secure a place in the will and then off with them! Well, I won't have it.

Miss Havisham *paces angrily and arrives at the dinner table.*

The next time they see me shall be at my funeral. When I am dead I shall be laid here – in the bride's dress on the bride's table! There will be Matthew's place – at my head! And there, Sarah beside him! And at my flank, Camilla, the greedy sow! And there, Raymond, that insipid husband of hers! And at my feet, Georgiana!

Miss Havisham *wheels around and continues to rant at* **Pip** *and* **Estella**. **Estella** *rolls her eyes, used to this behaviour.* **Pip** *is frozen in terror.*

Miss Havisham   I shall have place cards made up, so they know where to take their stations when they come to feast on me!

Miss Havisham *flings the birthday card into the corner of the room. She gathers herself and turns to face* **Pip** *once again.*

Miss Havisham   I do not allow my birthday to be spoken of.

Pip   I see.

Miss Havisham *considers* **Pip**.

Miss Havisham   Come with me, young man.

Pip *and* **Estella** *watch* **Miss Havisham** *go through to the next room. Slowly* **Pip** *turns to* **Estella**, *realisation dawning on him.*

Pip   You slapped my face.

Estella   I was saving you from yourself.

Pip   It hurt.

Estella   Would you like to kiss me?

Estella *leans close to* **Pip**.

Pip   Why?

Estella   Well, Fink, would you?

Pip *gingerly approaches* **Estella** *and kisses her lips.* **Estella** *stares back at him.*

Estella   Am I pretty?

Pip   Yes.

Estella   So pretty you could cry?

Pip   No.

Estella   You're not going to cry? Your eyes look wet. I think your lip is quivering.

Pip   I will never cry for you again.

Pip *stares* **Estella** *down, trying to look as convincing as possible, then turns and marches off after* **Miss Havisham**.

Estella *smiles, exits the other way.*

Miss Havisham *reappears,* **Pip** *follows her.*

Miss Havisham   What kept you?

Pip   Estella . . . she . . . well, she let me kiss her.

Miss Havisham   A kiss goodbye, most likely.

Pip   Goodbye?

Miss Havisham   Estella leaves tomorrow. She is to study art in Paris.

Pip   What, in France? For how long?

Miss Havisham   Long enough. As such, I have no more use for you.

Pip   I suppose not.

Miss Havisham *considers* **Pip**.

Miss Havisham   Your mother is a police officer, is she not?

Pip   Yes, Miss Havisham.

Miss Havisham   Do you ever think of following in her footsteps?

Pip   No. No disrespect, but it's a horrible job. She comes home in a proper state sometimes. And some of the people she works with . . .

Miss Havisham   Not for the likes of you. Do you contribute to the household?

Pip   I've been doing Saturdays in the big supermarket. Mum doesn't . . . we need the money.

Miss Havisham   Yes.

Miss Havisham *produces an envelope and hands it to* **Pip**. **Pip** *puts it in his pocket.*

Miss Havisham   Take this to your mother. You have been a good boy here, and that is your reward. Of course, as a good boy you should expect no other and no more. Now, leave.

Pip   Now? Should . . . should I come back sometime?

Miss Havisham   No. Constable Gargery is your only master now.

Miss Havisham *leaves, leaving* **Pip** *on his own.*

Pip *tries to go, but is frozen in his tracks.*

Pip   Paris . . .

Pip *tries to hold back tears, fails. He smacks his own forehead, berating himself for his stupid infatuation and his lack of dignity.*

Suddenly **Herbert Pocket**, *currently 20, appears, passing through, and spots* **Pip**.

Herbert   What ho. Something the matter, little man?

Pip *wheels around and wipes his eyes, embarrassed to have been caught crying.*

Pip   Who you calling little man? What you looking at anyway?

Herbert   I'm looking at a little crying man and wondering whether anything's the matter.

Pip *runs up and punches* **Herbert** *in the face.* **Herbert** *recoils, hurt, but laughing.*

Herbert   Phwoar! Quite a right hook you've got on you, little man. Learn to fight at school, did you? Good man.

Herbert *puts his dukes up playfully.*

Come on, then, let's see if you can hit me again.

Pip   What are you doing here?

Herbert   Come on, my lad, this is a boxing match, not an interview. See if you can land another punch!

Herbert *feints a punch towards* **Pip**, *who leans back, then hits* **Herbert** *again.* **Herbert** *is knocked to the ground.*

Herbert   Ha! What an arm! You ought to learn to control that temper, though, it's most unbecoming.

Pip   Who asked you?

Herbert   Ha! That's all for me. Nice to meet you, little man. Stay out of bother, won't you?

Herbert *walks off, staggering slightly, rubbing his chin.*

Pip, *somewhat baffled, rubs his fist and leaves for home.*

Nine

Jo's *flat, that evening.* **Jo** *and* **Biddy** *are in the kitchen.*

Jo   So why not? I thought you liked books.

Biddy   Yeah, but three years.

Jo   You've still got sixth form to get through, anyway, and I'm sure your aunt can help you with the money if you need it.

Pip *enters, still shaken.*

Jo   Pip! How was Miss Havisham's?

Pip   Fine.

Biddy   What's wrong?

Pip   They don't want me back any more.

Jo   What, why?

Jo *becomes suddenly severe.*

What did you do?

Pip   Nothing. Estella's going to Paris.

Jo   Oh. Pip, I'm sorry.

Pip   Didn't like it there anyway. Oh, this is for you.

Pip *hands* **Jo** *the envelope.*

Jo   What is it?

Pip   Didn't look.

Pip *sits next to* **Biddy**, *but doesn't look at her.* **Biddy** *regards him with sympathy.*

Jo *opens the envelope.*

Biddy   You okay?

Pip   Fine.

Jo   Pip, there's at least five thousand quid in here.

Biddy   Really?

Jo   Where did you get this? You didn't steal it, did you!?

Pip   No!

Jo   DID YOU?

Pip   No, Mum, it's from Miss Havisham! She told me to give it to you! She said it was my reward.

Jo   Well. Now that's a different story.

Pip   'For being a good boy.'

Biddy   Pip, that's great!

Jo   We can stop worrying about the water bill, anyway. And the council tax! Well, well, well, who'd have thought it.

Jo *embraces* **Pip**, *kisses him on the cheek. He is unmoved.*

Jo   Let me put this somewhere safe. See, Pip, you can't be that stupid.

Jo *exits.* **Pip** *sits sulking.* **Biddy** *tries to bring him out of himself.*

Biddy   Five grand. That'll be a big help. Aren't you happy?

Pip   It won't help.

Biddy   Yes it will, you heard your mum.

Pip   It's not enough to change our lives. It's just enough to keep them the same for a bit.

Biddy   What do you want changed so much?

Pip   We'll still be stuck living here. I'll get a proper job, somewhere. Mum'll keep working till she retires. I might meet a girl, someone local, someone convenient. Someone who doesn't mind me. Maybe we'll have kids. And I won't be able to give them anything better, either.

Biddy   Better?

Pip   And I'll always be rough and stupid.

Biddy   Who says you're rough and stupid?

Pip   Estella, the girl lives with Miss Havisham. She is more beautiful than any girl's ever been. And I'm in love with her.

Biddy   I see.

Pip   I wish I'd never seen her. I wish I'd never seen Satis House. I wish I could be happy with school and my flat and getting by. With you and Mum. I could have done a lot worse than falling in love with you. Do you think I'd have been good enough?

Biddy   I expect so. I'm not over-particular.

Pip   I'd have been happier. Do you know what it feels like to be ashamed of your own home?

Biddy   Ashamed . . .? So you want money and power and a fancy place to live because of Estella?

Pip   Yeah.

Biddy   Do you want that to get back at her, or to get in with her?

Pip   I don't know.

Biddy *rises, she's becoming irritated by this.*

Biddy   Because if it's to get back at her, I'd say – but I'm sure you know best – you could do that better by forgetting all about her. And if it's to get in with her, I'd say – and I'm sure you know best – she isn't worth it in the first place.

Pip   You're right, Biddy. You're always right. But there's nothing I can do. I love her, and there's nothing I can do.

Pip *runs his hands through his hair and grips it in thick bunches. He sobs.*

Biddy *sees this and cools, her irritation dissipates into pity. She walks around behind* **Pip**, *puts her hands over his and gently prises them away from his head. He calms down, sniffs, stops crying, gathers himself.*

Biddy   There's only one thing I can be happy about in all this, Pip, and it's that you trusted me with it.

Pip   Of course I trust you. I'll always tell you everything.

Biddy   Until you're rich and famous.

Pip   Ha! Snf. Until I'm rich and famous. But that will never happen, so it's always.

Biddy   You never know.

Pip   No. Trust me. Check back with me when I'm twenty and I'll still be mopping up baby vomit in the dairy aisle.

Biddy *leaves to join* **Jo**.

When she leaves, an incredibly dull voice comes through what sounds like a shopping centre tannoy. It takes **Pip** *forward four years to the next scene.*

Tannoy Voice   Clean-up in the dairy aisle, could we have a member of staff to the dairy aisle, there has been an incident with an infant.

Pip   Not again.

Ten

Four years later. **Pip** *is now 20.*

Pip *wakes up from the previous scene and throws on his shop assistant apron. A company member throws him a mop, with which he furiously scrubs the floor, muttering to himself. After a few seconds of scrubbing, he flings aside the broom and the apron with disdain.*

Pip   They should just bring the babies in sick bags and pour them out when they get home.

Biddy *appears, now 21.*

Biddy   I hope there are holes in the bags, in your scheme.

Pip   Doesn't bother me either way. How was school?

Biddy   Fine. 7M were a bit rowdy but Mister Wopsle handled it.

Pip   They given you anything more interesting than collecting exercise books?

Biddy   Collecting exercise books has its charms.

Pip   So no, then.

Biddy   They given you anything more interesting than spillages?

Pip   Blue Boar again?

Biddy   Yep. Orlick's invited himself.

Pip   Great.

Biddy   You never know. Maybe he's turned a page.

Pip   And he'll be . . . polite?

Biddy   Charming.

Pip   Witty, even.

Pip *and* **Biddy** *turn into the next scene, straight into. . .*

Eleven

The Blue Boar pub, that evening. **Jo**, **Biddy**, **Pip** *and* **Orlick** *all sit around the table,* **Orlick** *is mid-flow, cackling at his own story. He has brought today's edition of the local paper, a low-rent rag.*

Orlick   So we yank the door off the bog and have to drag him out to the car by his scalp. Nightmare! And I'll tell you what, if you've ever seen a filthier pub toilet I'll pull off my left bollock and you can take it home with you!

Orlick *finishes his pint, then looks offstage to the landlord.*

Same again and some pork scratchings, William mate, lovely.

Jo   Charming, Constable.

Biddy   Witty, I'd have said.

Pip   Very.

Orlick   And that's not the worst of it! Some of the buggers we have to deal with in this line of work . . . take that dirty sod up the road, the one in the paper – does in his wife in the middle of the night with the house all locked up, no way in, drops the knife in the laundry basket, blood all over the shop and he's still got the nerve to plead not guilty!

Biddy   Do we have to talk about this now?

Pip   Seems so.

Orlick   He's guilty as sin, and you can take that as my professional opinion.

At some point in **Orlick**'s *rant,* **Mister Jaggers**, *44, has appeared. He calls* **Orlick** *out.*

Jaggers   And your professional opinion is settled, then, is it?

Orlick *looks with surprise to the newcomer. The room goes silent.*

Orlick   Uh, yeah, yeah, it is. Who wants to know?

Jaggers   Were you the arresting officer on the scene?

Orlick   No, uh, not me, personally . . . but it's all there in the paper.

Jaggers   In the paper. That being the paper on the table.

Orlick   Well, yeah, I read it just now.

Jaggers   I am not interested in what you 'read just now', Officer, you might read the National Anthem backwards if it makes you happy, and perhaps you have done at some point in your life. But since you are such a conscientious upholder of the law, no doubt you noted every detail of the case?

Orlick   Yes. Yeah, I'd say so.

Jaggers   Then you will have read about the mysterious absence of the back door key?

Orlick   The what?

Jaggers   Open the paper and follow the article to the bottom. All the way to the end, sir.

Orlick *does as he's told, finds the right passage.*

Jaggers   You will notice that while all escape routes to the house were locked, there was no sign of the back door key anywhere inside the house, suggesting the possibility that the true murderer might have escaped, locking the back door behind them to cover their tracks, is that not so?

Orlick   Not in exactly those words.

Jaggers   But with exactly that meaning?

Orlick   Yeah. S'pose so.

Jaggers *addresses the others assembled at the table, and the audience, standing in for the other patrons of the Boar.*

Jaggers   I ask you, ladies and gentlemen, what you make of the conscience of a man who can lay his head on his pillow having so condemned a fellow human being, based solely on the evidence of an inflammatory tabloid headline.

Orlick *stares, stricken.* **Pip** *and* **Biddy** *are enjoying this tremendously, thrilled by the arrival of the stranger in the pub.*

Jaggers   Now, based on the information I have been given, one of you gathered here is a Josephine – or Jo – Gargery. I have been told that this young lady is a Sergeant in the Kent Police, which leads me to believe that this Jo is you, Officer?

Jo   That's me, right enough.

Jaggers   You, Sergeant Gargery, have a son by the name of Pip, is that right?

Jo   I do.

Jaggers   Is Pip here?

Pip, *hardly able to contain his excitement and terror, leaps out of his chair.*

Pip   Yes! I mean, that's me. Sir.

Jaggers   Come here.

Pip *walks over to* **Jaggers**, *who evaluates him.* **Jo** *stands up and moves around the table, concerned for* **Pip**.

Jo   What's all this about?

Jaggers   My name is Mister Jaggers, I am a Professor of Law at the London School of Economics and have come here to deliver a message to you regarding your son – namely, that he has great expectations.

Pip *looks shellshocked, as does* **Biddy**. **Orlick** *glowers with jealous rage.*

Jo   And what the bloody hell is that supposed to mean?

Jaggers   It means, Sergeant, that young Pip has been granted full funding and a place to study a Bachelor's in Law at my school.

Biddy   Pip!

Jaggers And that his accommodation and travel expenses are to be covered as well. In addition to which, he is to be granted a very generous allowance. His benefactor has given me the responsibility of divvying out this allowance, and of overseeing his education.

Jo Who on earth –

Jaggers – On two conditions.

Pip What conditions?

Jaggers Firstly, that he shall never know the identity of his benefactor, until such time as that benefactor thinks it right and proper, whenever that shall be. And secondly, that you shall always retain the name of Pip, whatever circumstance comes to pass. I trust you have no complaints about either of these conditions?

Pip No, sir.

Jaggers Attaboy. Of course, you are expected to live up to these expectations, which are that you shall better yourself, that you shall work hard, and learn, and live in service of the letter of the Law. To live a noble life, in short. Are you prepared to assume such a responsibility?

Pip Well, Mister Jaggers, I've always wanted . . .

Jaggers Never mind what you've always wanted, boy. Stick to the record. If you want it now, that is enough. Are you prepared to take up this scholarship immediately?

Pip Yes. I am.

Jaggers Then I will see you at matriculation two Mondays from now. I will be in touch soon regarding your accommodation and your bank details.

Pip I . . . I don't have a bank account.

Jaggers Open one. It will soon come under some considerable strain.

Jaggers *turns and storms out.* **Biddy** *leaps up and runs to* **Pip**, *throwing her arms around him and kissing him on the cheek.*

Orlick *stands up and slumps out towards the exit, stopping only to turn and shoot* **Pip** *a filthy look.*

Jo *leads* **Pip** *and* **Biddy** *back to the table, bringing them into the next scene.*

Twelve

Jo*'s flat, late that night, after much revelry in the pub.* **Pip** *and* **Biddy** *carry* **Jo** *over to a chair by the kitchen table. All three are tipsy at this point. It is that time of the night when talk flows freely, perhaps too freely.*

Jo   My son! My little baby! A gen'leman of fortune, eh?

Jo *ruffles* **Pip***'s hair.*

Pip   That's me.

Jo   Soon you'll forget all about this flat and Rochester and your old mum and everything and move on to pastures greener.

Jo *suppresses a small burp.*

Pip   No, Mum, of course not!

Jo   Ah, s'a way of the world. Phwoo, my head's spinning.

Biddy   You alright getting to bed, Jo?

Jo   Fanks, Biddy, I'm right as rain, nothing a good night's sleep won't cure.

Jo *stands up with some slight difficulty and goes over to* **Pip**. *She pats his cheeks affectionately, but slightly too hard.*

Jo   You'll be gone soon.

Pip   In a couple of weeks.

Jo   They'll soon go. They'll soon go.

Jo *staggers out to bed.* **Pip** *sits down by the table.*

Pip   Gonna miss you, Biddy.

Biddy   You won't. You'll go make new friends and find new places, and you won't think of us back here at all.

Pip   Naah! I'll make it in London and send for everyone. And we'll have a flat like this, only fi – no, SIX times the size . . . and without any mice . . . or woodlice.

Pip *spots and smashes a woodlouse on the table with his fist.*

Got 'im. An' I'll never forget you, Biddy, not ever.

Biddy   And not Jo, either?

Pip   No! No, course not! You'll look after her while I'm away, right? Then one day, we'll all go to London together and ride around in black cabs everywhere and when people say 'hello', we'll say 'good day, my fine fellow' and give them a quid.

Biddy   Careful, you'll get poor again quick doing that.

Pip   And Mum won't have to work in the police, never again.

Biddy   No?

Pip   And you won't have to be a teacher, either.

Biddy   Oh, won't I?

Pip   Not if you don't want to.

Biddy   What if I do want to?

Pip   Suit yourself.

Biddy   Jo might like being a police officer, you don't know.

Pip   Come on.

Biddy   Well. I hope this isn't the new Pip. Pip with money. All of a sudden public services are beneath him.

Pip *looks suspiciously at* **Biddy**.

Pip   Are you jealous?

Biddy   Jealous!

Pip   It's not a very nice side of human nature, that's all.

Biddy *goes to get her coat and puts it on over the following parting shot.*

Biddy   Whether you like my nature or not, I'll certainly take care of Jo while you're away. And whatever opinion of me you take with you, it won't change how I remember you.

Pip   Biddy . . .

Biddy   But no lawyer ought to be unjust, all the same.

Exit **Biddy**.

Pip *watches her go, troubled. He shakes off the drunkenness of the scene and slaps his own face to wake himself up. He puts on a tie and a smart jacket and suddenly he's sober and ready for the next scene.*

Thirteen

Satis House, two weeks later. **Miss Havisham** *approaches cautiously.*

Miss Havisham   Is it Pip?

Pip   Yes, Miss Havisham.

Miss Havisham *straightens* **Pip**'s *collar and tie, caring nothing for his personal space.*

Miss Havisham   What a pretty figure you make.

Pip   I've been done a very big favour since I last saw you, Miss Havisham. And . . . I'm very grateful for it.

Miss Havisham   I'm sure you are.

Pip   No, I want you to know . . . I'm very grateful to . . . whoever thinks I deserve it.

Miss Havisham   Yes, yes, of course. Mister Jaggers has told me all about it. He manages my affairs, you see.

Pip   Right.

Miss Havisham   He tells me you are off to London tomorrow, is that right?

Pip   Yes, Miss Havisham.

Miss Havisham   And you are sponsored by some rich person?

Pip   Yes.

Miss Havisham   Not named.

Pip   No.

Miss Havisham   And Mister Jaggers will be overseeing your progress?

Pip   Yes, Miss Havisham.

Miss Havisham   Well! Then you have a promising career ahead of you. Be good – deserve it – and abide by Mister Jaggers's instructions.

Pip   Yes, Miss Havisham.

Miss Havisham *begins to retreat into the house.*

Pip   I would have liked to say goodbye to Estella, as well.

Miss Havisham *turns slowly around, delighted to hear* **Pip** *say her name.*

Miss Havisham   Yes. A shame, isn't it? She's in Berlin, now. A sculptor of some repute, and quite the socialite, by all accounts. It's said that she has become even more elegant, even more beautiful. Her contemporaries fall at her feet, men and women alike. But then, that's Berlin for you.

Pip   I see.

Miss Havisham *comes closer to* **Pip** *and stares right into his eyes. It is unclear whether the following words are spoken aloud, or are the product of some sort of hypnosis.*

Miss Havisham   Love her, Pip. If she wounds you, love her! If she favours you, love her! If she tears your heart to pieces – and as it gets older and stronger it will tear deeper – love her!

Pip *stares back.*

Miss Havisham   But enough of Estella – it's time to say goodbye, Pip. You will always be my little Pip, won't you?

Pip   Yes, Miss Havisham.

Miss Havisham *exits back into Satis House.*

Pip *takes a deep breath and sighs it out, steeling himself for the journey ahead.*

Fourteen

Pip*'s journey to London is communicated through company movement. The whole company swarms* **Pip***, running around a train station. Along the way, one of them gives* **Pip** *his suitcase, which he clutches tightly. The announcer comes over the tannoy, the crowd freezes to listen.*

Announcer   The ten-twenty-eight train to London Victoria is now arriving at platform two.

This announcement sends the crowd bustling across the stage, taking **Pip** *with them. The crowd bustles and argues as it goes, with rough shouts of 'Watch it' and 'Out of the way'.*

The announcer is now the voiceover on an Underground train.

Announcer   The next station is Pimlico.

The crowd bustles across stage again to the exit, taking **Pip** *with them, but suddenly their cries are in clipped RP accents, with shouts of 'Oh, terribly sorry' and passive-aggressive murmurs of 'Pardon me'.*

The crowd leaves the stage, leaving **Pip** *alone, looking dazed. He walks to centre-stage, now the living room of* **Herbert***'s flat in Pimlico, and puts down his case.*

Pip   Hello? Anyone home?

Herbert*'s voice comes from just offstage.*

Herbert   Oh, hello! It must be Mister Pirrip, mustn't it?

Pip   Pip, yeah.

Herbert*, 24, bustles across the stage, carrying books and dirty mugs, rearranging his things. He doesn't look at* **Pip** *at all as he hurries around.* **Pip***, sensing his preoccupation, instead looks around the flat.*

Herbert   Pip. I don't like that very much. We'll have to come up with some kind of familiar greeting very quickly or else we'll never be friends. How was the trip?

Pip   Busy. This place is really nice.

Herbert   I'm glad you like it! Saves you the weeks of acclimatising yourself to disappointment. Yours is the smaller bedroom.

Pip   Oh, that's fine, I –

Pip *and* **Herbert** *bump into each other in their travels across the living room. The two of them look directly at each other for the first time.*

Herbert   My God! Little man!

Pip   You! Didn't I punch you in the face once?

They both burst out laughing.

Herbert   The idea of it being you! The idea of it being YOU!

Pip   I don't believe it. What are you doing here?

Herbert   I live here.

Pip   Alright, then what were you doing at Miss Havisham's place?

Herbert   Oh, my Aunt Sarah sent me to deliver a birthday card for Miss Havisham.

Pip   Ah.

Herbert   She didn't take it very well.

Pip   No, she didn't.

Herbert   But family grievances can wait – for the moment we have two important questions to address. Firstly, where are we having dinner? Secondly, what am I going to call you?

Pip   Pip's fine, honest.

Herbert   Fine for you, maybe, but I'm afraid it does nothing for me.

Pip   Maybe Philip?

Herbert   Eugh, even worse. Sounds like an ill-fated boy in a cautionary tale. Mister Jaggers told me that you were working in a supermarket back in Rochester, isn't that right?

Pip   Uh, yes, mostly Saturdays, but whatever shifts I could get.

Herbert   Then that settles it.

Pip   It does?

Herbert   Yes! I'll call you Billy.

Pip   Billy?

Herbert   Like Billy Bragg. The Saturday Boy. 'I lied to myself about the chances I wasted!' No?

Pip   'Fraid not.

Herbert   Well, at any rate, to me you shall always be Billy.

Pip   Billy. Alright. Will you tell me your name, or do I have to make one up as well?

Herbert   Oh! Silly me, of course. Herbert. Herbert Pocket.

Herbert *extends a hand.* **Pip** *shakes it.*

Pip   So what about the first question, then?

Herbert   I know just the place.

A company member storms onto stage in character as an Italian waiter with an outrageously thick accent, bringing us into the next scene.

Fifteen

The Italian waiter claps his hands, transforming **Herbert***'s flat into an upscale Italian restaurant. Other company members lay the table, setting out plates, knives, forks, white wine, glasses and napkins for* **Pip** *and* **Herbert**. **Pip** *is put off by his intense professional friendliness.*

Waiter   Giuseppe! More bread sticks for my wonderful friends! So sorry for your wait, my fine gentlemen, your table is ready, buon appetito!

Pip   Tha – thank you?

Waiter   PREGO!

Herbert   So where was I?

Pip   I think you were talking about Estella?

Herbert   Oh, yes. Frightful girl. Horrible.

Pip *is shocked by this, tries to disguise his anger.*

Pip   Really?

Herbert Oh yes, brought up by Miss Havisham to wreak some terrible vengeance on every man who ever comes within fifty feet of her.

Pip She's not . . . THAT bad.

Herbert She is, trust me. As if it wasn't bad enough that my aunt was trying to set me up with some teenager – stupid idea, rebuilding burnt bridges or something – she turned out to be the most spiteful little brat. Still, can't blame her too much, with no parents around and only that old shut-in for company and I only break from my story, Billy, to tell you that white wine is best held by the stem, not the bulb of the glass.

Pip Oh, sorry.

Herbert Not at all, old chap.

Pip So why would Miss Havisham want her to hurt anyone?

Herbert Broken heart, of course! Sad story, really, she was abandoned at the altar.

Pip That explains a few things.

Pip *tucks his napkin into his collar.*

Herbert No! Not at the altar, not quite. In fact, she was in Satis House, just getting in the car, when she received the message. One of the groom's mob brought it over, some solider. She had just got into her wedding dress when she got the news and I only pause for a moment, Billy, to suggest that in places like this, the napkin is best worn on the lap, rather than tucked in.

Pip Oh, sorry.

Herbert Not at all, old chap. And here's the spooky thing – did you notice the clocks in her place?

Pip They . . . don't work?

Herbert   Precisely! Broken! Smashed in at exactly twenty to nine – the very moment she was told that her fiancé had flown the coop. She was utterly humiliated. She sent away the dress fitter, all of her bridesmaids – my mother included – and since that very instant she has never set foot outside the house.

Pip   That's ludicrous.

Herbert   It's God's honest truth.

Pip   All over one bloke?

Herbert   It's never really about one bloke, though, is it? It's a lifetime of family expectation, a spoiled and stifled upbringing, too much money and not enough sense. Years of mummy and daddy needling you, 'when are you going to find a nice boy, you're not getting any younger'. Finally you find a strapping, upstanding, handsome young military type who says he loves every inch of you, only for him to do a runner at the last minute? And I only pause from my story, Billy, to ask . . .

Pip   Yes?

Herbert   Could you pass the wine?

Pip   Oh. Sure.

Pip *passes* **Herbert** *the bottle of wine.* **Herbert** *refills his glass as he continues.*

Herbert   A proud person can't survive a public embarrassment like that, and Miss Havisham more than proves it.

Pip   So how does Estella fit into all this? Miss Havisham adopted her, didn't she?

Herbert   Supposedly, though I've no idea if it's ever been legally endorsed. I can't imagine what social worker would ever sign off on that.

Pip   Did she adopt her before the wedding day?

Herbert   Oh, God no, first I heard of Estella was years after, she just sort of turned up. Left in a basket in the reeds, perhaps?

Pip   I don't get it.

Herbert   Like Moses, Billy, destined to lead us to the promised land. Though in Estella's case, more likely to lead us back to Pharaoh.

Pip   Cool. So . . . you teach at LSE?

Herbert   Sort of. Junior Research Fellow. Keeps me going. I'm just treading water until I can go into private practice. But Jesus, the expense. Never mind finding the office, do you know how much it costs just to have one of those little brass plates engraved? It's –

Suddenly **Bentley Drummle**, *24, appears, tipsy, an insidious slur in his voice.*

Drummle   Well, look whose ship's lights I see on the horizon!

Herbert   Oh God.

Drummle   Pocket! Herbert Pocket! Fancy seeing a rascal like you here.

Drummle *stomps over and smacks* **Herbert** *on the back a bit too hard.*

Herbert   Hello, Drummle.

Drummle *inspects the wine.*

Drummle   God, 'Blossom Valley'. Well, long as it's good enough for Mister Tesco.

Drummle *notices* **Pip**.

Drummle   I hope I'm not interrupting anything important, Herbert. Where did you pick him up, by the school gates?

Pip   Hang on a minute –

Herbert He's just teasing. Bentley, this is Mister Philip Pirrip, new intake at LSE, just arrived in town.

Pip *dubiously extends a hand.*

Pip Pip.

Drummle *sneers.*

Drummle If you insist. I like your shirt. What is that, Massimo Dutti?

Pip Uh, TK Maxx.

Drummle I see. How daring!

Herbert What brings you out of the shadows, Drummle?

Drummle Oh, just taking the young lady out for a night on the town.

Herbert Which one's this?

Drummle Which one! Tania! Always Tania. Of course Tania.

Herbert Of course Tania.

Drummle In fact, I'm neglecting her terribly. I'll leave you lovebirds to it. See you in the designated staff common area, Pocket. Toodle-bye.

Drummle *strides away in a loathsomely self-regarding, catwalk-esque manner. Smug smile, shoulders back, head held high, very aware that he looks absolutely brilliant.*

Herbert So that's Drummle.

Pip Are there lots of him in London?

Herbert More than I like to think.

Pip He's amazing.

Herbert How so?

Pip   I've only known him for two minutes, but literally everything about him makes me want to kick him in the head.

Herbert *laughs.*

Herbert   Welcome to London, Billy.

Herbert *raises his glass.* **Pip** *starts to do the same, holding his glass by the bulb. He stops himself, grips the stem of the glass instead, then clinks glasses with* **Herbert**.

Herbert *and* **Pip** *leave, company clears the glasses and chairs, leaving only the table, positioned centre-stage. It becomes the front desk in a lecture hall.*

Sixteen

Pip *takes a seat in the audience just in time for* **Mister Jaggers** *to appear behind the desk. The rest of the company has disappeared. He bangs his fist on the table to silence anybody still talking in the audience, taking them to a lecture hall in LSE.*

Jaggers   A little quiet, please, ladies and gentlemen.

You think you know everything, don't you? Of course you do. You knew enough to survive your schooling, enough to survive your UCAS applications and finally, enough to make it here. Of course, studying at the London School of Economics and Political Science is a tremendous honour, which I'm sure all of you will take very seriously. Do you know what you need to know to get to where you are now?

Nothing. You need know nothing, and you know nothing now. If I threw a dart in this room, now, I guarantee you it will hit somebody who is in danger of failing this course. None of you is safe, not if you lose sight of your studies, or if you take your place here for granted for even a second.

I believe in the letter of the Law. There are thousands, millions of people out there – vulnerable people, desperate people, people who never had the options you have – who will one day rely on somebody like you for justice. You may not like them, in fact, if you're anything like me, you'll despise almost all of them, but they are human beings, and every human being, however repellent, deserves justice. You are sitting here now because you understand this, or at least because you made a very good show of understanding it in your interview.

If any one of you fails to live up to this ideal, through laziness, arrogance or your own smug sense of superiority, I will have you thrown naked from the front gates of this establishment, tattooed with the legend 'I forgot who I am'.

Welcome to your Bachelor of Laws.

Pip *leads a round of applause in the audience.*

Jaggers *turns and takes a seat behind the table, which becomes his desk.*

Pip *leaves the audience and sits opposite him for his tutorial.*

Jaggers   Mister Pirrip. No doubt you have some questions for me.

Pip   A few, Professor.

Jaggers   Please, call me Mister Jaggers, I like to be reminded that I work in education as infrequently as possible.

Pip   Yes, Mister Jaggers.

Jaggers   So. Questions.

Pip   Well, there's just one, really, which I can't stop thinking about, ever since you first came to find me in the Blue Boar.

Jaggers   And that question is?

Pip   Why am I here?

Jaggers   No, no, no. A very poorly-phrased question. At best it provokes a clinical account of the nature of reproductive biology, and at worst, it makes me think you are trying to divine the identity of your benefactor, which as I very clearly told you –

Pip   No, I get that, and of course I'll play by the rules, but . . . why me? Here? I never even applied.

Jaggers   To go into too much detail would give you clues enough to begin making deductions. You don't fool me, Mister Pirrip. You are gifted with more intelligence than you let on, and unless I miss my mark, and I never do, you have become used to employing this feigned ignorance to gain the confidence of others.

Pip   I'm sorry, Mister Jaggers, I never meant to –

Jaggers   I'm not accusing you of doing so wilfully, but it's evidently a habit you have got into, and not a very pleasant one. You'd do well to cast it off as quickly as possible. There's no time for playing dumb here.

Besides, you had the requisite A-levels to study here, if only barely, and there was a space left through Clearing.

Pip   But who would ever do all this for me, I've no idea.

Jaggers   There's that nasty habit of yours again. Forgive me if I gag on my rising bile at any point, I swear it's a purely involuntary reaction.

Pip   You must understand how hard it is, not knowing.

Jaggers   I'm sure it's pure agony, and yet my hands are tied. Be satisfied with this – someone, no matter who, believed in you, and believed well enough to go to the trouble of ensuring you a place at this institution, once the opportunity presented itself. Not to mention the amount of money they've put up.

Pip   God, the money.

Jaggers   Don't waste another second worrying about who or why or how much, Mister Pirrip, just get to work proving that your benefactor's belief was not ill-placed.

Pip   Yes. Of course, yes.

Jaggers   Has the first instalment of your allowance arrived in your account yet?

Pip *remembers the number of zeroes he saw on his bank balance that morning.*

Pip   It has.

Jaggers   Then you may be satisfied with that as well.

Mister Jaggers *goes to leave, then stops himself. He consults a note on his desk.*

Oh, it nearly slipped my mind. An acquaintance of mine got in touch with a message for you. Miss Havisham, if that name means anything to you.

Pip   Miss Havisham? Yes. Yes, of course!

Jaggers   She wants you to do a delivery job for her.

Pip   A delivery job.

Jaggers   Yes, you are to deliver her ward, Miss Estella, from Satis House to Charing Cross. She is moving back to England next week. Are you alright, my boy? You look rather pale.

Pip   She's back from Berlin?

Jaggers   Indeed. Apparently she's trying to break England.

Mister Jaggers *leaves. All* **Pip**'s *memories of* **Estella** *suddenly become more vivid, he is swarmed by them.*

Pip   I'm sure she'll manage.

Blackout.

Interval.

Seventeen

Satis House. **Estella**, *now 20, glides onto stage, even more beautiful than before, carrying her suitcase, dressed far too well for a train journey. There is an unflappable coolness to her demeanour, the result of several years of unflattering self-discoveries.*

Miss Havisham, *now 56, follows her.*

Miss Havisham   To leave me here, alone, mere days after returning! What, are you tired of me?!

Estella   Just a little tired of myself, mother.

Miss Havisham   Don't call me that! How can you be so cold?

Estella   You're calling me cold? You?

Miss Havisham   Aren't you?

Estella   You should know. You made me what I am. The praise is yours, the blame is yours. Take the success, take the failure. In short, take me.

Miss Havisham   Oh, look at her! Standing in the very house where I took her in! Where I gave her everything she could ever need! Where I reared her!

Pip *enters, dressed up for* **Estella**. *He stands at the extreme of the stage, having overheard their conversation so far, waiting respectfully, feeling uncomfortable at having to witness this argument.*

Estella   Mother.

Miss Havisham   I said don't CALL me tha –

Estella   Mother by adoption, then. I have said many times, I owe you everything. Everything I have is yours. Everything you ever gave me, you are free to have back again, whenever you choose it. What else can I offer you?

Miss Havisham   Love! Your love!

Estella   I cannot give you what you never gave me. I can't recreate something I was never shown.

Miss Havisham   Did I never show her love! How can you be so proud? So proud!

Estella   Who taught me to be proud?

Miss Havisham   So hard! So hard!

Estella   Who taught me to be hard? Who praised me when I learnt my lesson?

Miss Havisham   But to be cold and hard to me! To ME!

Miss Havisham *turns and runs away, further into the house. She howls and sobs theatrically as she goes, doing her best to punish* **Estella** *for her cruelty.*

Estella   Hello, Pip.

Pip   Estella. You look –

Estella   Let's go.

Estella *thrusts her suitcase into* **Pip**'s *hands.*

Pip   Okay.

The company swarms the stage again, back in the guise of the commuters. They angrily run to-and-fro, checking their watches, complaining about the delayed train, barging past each other.

Eighteen

Pip *struggles to keep up with* **Estella**, *who seems to glide through the chaos, untouched by the bustle.*

Announcer   The twelve-thirty train to London Victoria is now arriving at platform two.

The company leaves the swarm around **Pip** *and goes over to* **Estella**. *They produce two chairs and place them next to each other, sitting* **Estella** *down in one of them, eager to please her. 'There you are, Miss,' 'Is that comfy for you, Miss?' etc.*

Pip, *shellshocked, goes over to sit next to her on the train as the English landscape flies past through the window.*

Estella   You've changed, Pip.

Pip   Less ignorant?

Estella   Yes, I think I probably did say such a thing, once. I was not a very pleasant little creature. Making fun. Calling you names.

Pip   I could take it.

Estella   Have I changed?

Pip   Yes. At first I hardly recognised you, but sitting next to you here, now, it's clear you're still the same old Estella.

Estella   Not the old Estella, I hope. Not the insulting little girl that you wanted to get away from so badly.

Pip   I didn't mean it like that.

Estella   I think you did.

Pip   You could be very difficult to be around. Sometimes. I didn't think Miss Havisham would tell you that.

Estella   I don't mind. But you mustn't put so much trust in Miss Havisham. You didn't spend your every waking moment in that house, as I did. You didn't have your little wits sharpened by the whittling away of her razor tongue. You didn't have to listen to her lecturing you on the futility of love. You weren't reminded daily that to surrender your affection to another human being is death.

I'll always remember your fight.

Pip   Which fight?

Estella   I watched from a window of the house. You were on the front lawn when that Pocket boy approached you. You hit him.

Pip   Oh. Yes.

Estella   I don't know what kind of person I can have been, to watch the two of you fighting, and be so delighted by it. His aunt had tried to trick us into becoming friends. Luckily Miss Havisham was convinced that this was just another attempt by Sarah Pocket to worm her way back into the will, so he was sent away within minutes.

Pip   Pity. I live with Herbert now, we're good friends.

Estella   Herbert?

Pip   The Pocket boy, as you called him.

Estella   Oh. How strange. A good man?

Pip   Oh, yes. Nobody's enemy but –

Estella   Oh, please don't say nobody's enemy but his own, I can't stand people like that.

Pip   Then I'll hold off my judgement. You're going to be living in Dalston?

Estella   Yes. I found a patron of sorts in Berlin. An older lady, a painter. She's letting out part of her studio, and her spare room. She knows people in London, says she can get me exhibitions, spaces in shows, maybe an agent. She says I'm 'a singular, exciting new voice' in sculpting and that she just HAS to sponsor my continuing career. To be honest I suspect she's just in love with me.

Pip   Not the worst thing in the world, to be loved.

Estella   Not the worst.

Announcer   The next station is London Charing Cross.

The company swarms the stage again, clearing **Pip** *and* **Estella**'s *chairs, shoving* **Pip** *to the other side of the stage.* **Estella** *glides along behind them, unmoved.*

The company puts two chairs at an angle to each other, as if around a table in a cafe. They shove **Pip** *into one chair and thrust a coffee into his hand, 'Coffee for "Pip"?'*

Estella *sits gracefully down in the other chair. A company member kneels in front of her, holding out another takeaway coffee cup in their hand, 'Coffee for "Estella"?'* **Estella** *takes it, hardly noticing the company around them, and the company disbands and disappears.*

Estella   I forgot how terrible the coffee is in England.

Pip   Not like in Berlin?

Estella   No.

Pip   The day of the fight. Just before you left England. You let me kiss you.

Estella   A gift, given for the wrong reasons.

Pip   I didn't mind why you gave it.

Estella   I suspect it was an act of rebellion. Showing some kind of affection outside Miss Havisham's influence. But it wasn't real affection if it was done for my own good. I was just using you, the same way she used me.

Pip   I didn't mind being used.

Estella   You still won't take my warning.

Pip   You have to tell me what that warning is, if I'm supposed to take it.

Estella   I have no heart. Oh, I have a heart to be stabbed or shot in, I'm sure. And if it ceased to beat, I should cease to be. But there is no softness there. No sympathy. No sentiment.

Pip *opens his mouth to disagree.*

Estella   No! It's the truth. And if I'm going to see much of you in London, you have to get used to the idea at once. I have no tenderness. I have never given such a thing to anybody, and I don't suspect I'll ever have the ability.

Pip *looks at her, totally consumed by pity.*

Estella   What's the matter? Are you frightened?

Pip   I would be, if I believed what you just said.

Estella *shrugs.*

Estella   I tried.

Bentley Drummle *appears with an irritatingly small suitcase on wheels. He calls to* **Pip**.

Drummle   Pirrip! I say, Pirrip! Fancy running into a scoundrel like you here!

Pip   Oh no.

Drummle   And in the company of such a beguiling young lady.

Drummle *makes immediately for* **Estella** *and extends his hand.*

Drummle   Bentley Drummle. I suppose Pip's told you all about me.

Estella   Not a word, Mister Drummle.

Pip   We've had a lot to catch up on, Drummle. In fact, we were in the middle of –

Drummle   You old rogue, Pirrip, keeping the pretty ones to yourself.

Pip   You've got the wrong idea, Drummle.

Estella   Yes, Mister Drummle, Pip and I are old friends.

Drummle   Bentley, please, Miss . . .?

Estella   Estella.

Drummle   What a lovely name. Just passing through?

Estella   Moving in.

Drummle   How delightful.

Pip   What are YOU doing here, Drummle?

Drummle   Quick weekend away with the parentals at their place in the country. A rare couple of days without any National Trust tours scurrying about. We had the place to ourselves.

Pip   How lovely for you.

Drummle   What do you do when you're not drinking train station coffee, Estella?

Estella   I'm a sculptor, or trying to be.

Drummle   Creative type. Shoreditch?

Estella   Dalston.

Drummle   Near enough. Either way the coffee will be far superior. I'm over in Old Street, you must get in touch sometime. I'll show you the sights.

Drummle *gives* **Estella** *his card.*

Estella   I didn't realise you were a tour guide.

Drummle   I could be, if the mood took me.

Pip   Estella and I were just in the middle of a conversation, Drummle, if you don't mind.

Drummle   Sounds frightfully serious. Good luck with it. Estella, a pleasure.

Estella   Bentley.

Drummle *walks away in his catwalk model fashion.*

Estella   He's a character.

Pip   From a book I wouldn't want to read.

Estella   He's very good-looking.

Pip   He knows it. They call him the Spider. He can usually be found stringing up a web in the corner of a party, then lying in wait until a girl's left alone so he can pounce.

Estella   A man who knows what he wants.

Pip   I'd stay away from him, if I were you. He leaves a lot of broken hearts behind.

Estella   A dangerous man, then. If you have a heart to be broken.

Pause.

Pip   Are you going to be alright getting to Dalston Junction?

Estella I'll manage. It was very nice to see you again, Pip.

Pip You too! You too, uh. I'd like to . . . if you don't mind, once more . . .

Pip *tails off.* **Estella** *leans closer to* **Pip.**

Pip *nervously kisses her lips. It's colder and more formal than before.*

Pip Good luck in London. I hope you and Miss Havisham will make peace soon.

Estella I've promised to write to her. She wants to hear as much of my progress as possible.

Pip Personal or professional?

Estella Whatever she can get her hands on.

Estella *nods to* **Pip,** *then glides away.*

As soon as she is gone, **Pip** *sags, turns and walks away, completely in love.*

Nineteen

Herbert's *flat, later that afternoon.* **Herbert** *sits reading with a glass of wine.*

Pip *enters, still mired in heart-ache.*

Herbert Afternoon, Billy.

Pip Bit early, isn't it?

Herbert Yes, it most certainly is, mother. Want a glass?

Pip Not just now.

Herbert Everything alright, Billy? You look like you've seen a ghost.

Pip I have.

Herbert I know I'd want a drink if I were in your position.

Herbert *fetches the bottle of wine and an extra glass. He fills it and sets it down near* **Pip**, *who ignores it.*

Pip   I've got to tell you something, Herbert.

Herbert   Certainly.

Pip   It's about me . . . and someone else.

Herbert *looks at* **Pip** *attentively, waiting for him to continue.*

Pip   I love . . . I'm in love with Estella.

Herbert   Yes.

Pip   What do you mean 'yes'?

Herbert   I mean yes, and?

Pip   I'm pouring my heart out to you here, mate, and all you can say is 'yes'.

Herbert   Well what do you want me to say?

Pip   A little bit of surprise might be nice, any sort of ceremony to mark the occasion!

Herbert   But I already know! I've always known!

Pip   How? How do you know?

Herbert   From you, you idiot!

Pip   I never told you!

Herbert   You never tell me when you get a haircut either, but I still know it's happened! I could see it the second you walked in here, it was written all over your face! The way you clench your buttocks every time anybody mentions her name! You might as well have had a t-shirt made up, Billy! 'Keep Calm and I Love Estella'!

Pip   Alright, alright.

Herbert   What I want to know is, what are you going to do about it?

Pip I don't know. When I was a kid, she was worlds away from me. Now she's back and she's . . . impossible. She's like the sun. It hurts just to look at her. And now that we're in the same city, she feels further away than ever.

Herbert Haven't you come up in the world, yourself? Don't you move in more exciting circles now, like the ones she moves in?

Pip When I was the Saturday boy at least I knew who I was. Now I don't even know that.

Herbert If I had to venture a guess, I'd say 'a good fellow'.

Pip You think so?

Herbert Yes. A man in whom impetuosity and hesitation, boldness and diffidence, dreaming and action are curiously mixed.

Pip Sounds like every person I ever met.

Herbert Then call yourself that. A person.

Pip A very lucky person, who's done nothing to deserve his luck.

Herbert I'm going to make myself very unpleasant now, Billy, and I want you to prepare yourself.

Pip Do your worst.

Herbert I think you need to forget about her. I know that's like asking a fish to forget water, or a Conservative to forget Thatcher, and all that, but I think it's very important – for you – that you try. And start trying now.

Pip I see.

Herbert See. I told you I'd make myself unpleasant.

Pip You've done very well.

Herbert May I attempt to redeem myself?

Pip I think you'd better.

Herbert   Then I'd like to remind you of all the more important things you've got to worry about. Like this glass of wine, which I have to say you have been neglecting most gracelessly.

Pip *takes a drink, considers.*

Pip   I can't forget her. She's the only thing keeping me sane. Sometimes, thinking about everything I have to live up to, trying to be this new person, it's too much. The only way I can make sense of it all is the thought that somewhere down the line, this new life might somehow bring us together.

Herbert   Then might I suggest an alternate plan of action?

Pip   Anything.

Herbert   Throw yourself into your work. Whatever your motives, whatever it is that's steering you, you mustn't blow this now. You'll never forgive yourself.

Pip   You think that'll work?

Herbert   It's absolutely the best prescription for an ache in the heart. With any luck, it'll help you forget all about her. If not, you'll at least have something to show for your years of self-torture and chastity.

Yes, Billy, I'm certain. The best thing for you now is to bury your head in your studies, show Jaggers what you can do, and become the man your benefactor dreamed of when he or she set you off down this road.

Herbert *refills his and* **Pip**'s *glasses.*

Herbert   Starting tomorrow.

Herbert *and* **Pip** *clink glasses and down their drinks.*

Herbert *refills their glasses and they down them immediately.*

The company enters as a crowd of drunken revellers, handing **Pip** *and* **Herbert** *bottles of beer, then shot glasses, all of which they consume greedily.*

Thumping dance music kicks off as they drink and some clumsy, Friday night dancing begins. The music resolves itself into **Estella's** *voice, freezing* **Pip** *in his tracks – 'Do you still find me beautiful?' –* **Pip** *shakes it off and goes back to his drunken dancing.*

The company dissipates, leaving **Pip** *and* **Herbert** *to stagger back home,* **Herbert** *propping* **Pip** *up. He dumps* **Pip** *behind the table and pats his face affectionately, before staggering off to bed.* **Pip** *is out cold, a big dumb grin on his face.*

Twenty

Pip *wakes up with a start. His eyes widen at the sudden arrival of the hangover.*

Pip OH MY GOD.

Herbert *wanders into the room in a dressing gown. He puts two paracetamol and a glass of water in front of* **Pip** *at the desk, then drops a large hardback book in front of him.* **Pip** *winces at the noise it makes when it lands.*

Herbert To your studies, Mister Billy. We have a lot of laws in this country, and you've only got three years to learn what they all are.

Pip *looks up for mercy, his face creased with agony.*

Pip Starting tomorrow?

Herbert *consults his watch.*

Herbert Starting . . . now.

Herbert *exits.* **Pip** *sighs, takes the paracetamol and opens the book.*

Time accelerates, **Pip** *flips forward through half the book, making notes as he goes.* **Herbert** *reappears holding two glasses of wine.* **Pip** *waves him away, looking nauseous at the prospect of drink.* **Herbert** *shrugs, drinks both glasses, then skips merrily out the door.*

Pip *flips through the second half of the book, periodically typing manically on his laptop computer. Just as* **Pip** *triumphantly finishes* *the book, slamming the back cover down,* **Mister Jaggers** *drifts past and drops an even larger book on top of that one.* **Pip** *groans, wipes his brow, then opens the second book.*

Herbert *staggers back in, drunk again, pats* **Pip**'s *face as he passes and wanders off to bed.* **Pip** *flinches at the patting of his face, but otherwise his concentration is undisturbed.* **Pip** *continues to type, make notes and flip through the book.*

Herbert *reappears, in the throes of a tremendous hangover, dressed for work, cradling a briefcase. He takes two paracetamol with a huge swig of water and marches out the door.*

Many months have passed. **Pip**'s *studies are interrupted by a knock at the door.*

Pip Who is it?

Jo's *voice comes from outside the door.*

Jo Police! Open up!

Pip Police?

Pip *moves towards the front door.* **Jo** *appears, dressed in civvies.*

Pip Mum! Mum, what a . . . what a nice surprise! Come in!

Pip *throws his arms around* **Jo** *as an afterthought.*

Jo Well, well, well. Look at this place.

Pip Yes, isn't it nice?

Jo I'm sure it was before you got to it. Hard at work?

Pip Uh, yes, yes, I was.

Jo I'm sorry, Philip, I didn't mean to interrupt you.

Pip No, not at all, don't be ridiculous! Have a seat!

Jo *sits in a seat by the table.*

Jo Just wanted to see this exciting new life of yours for myself. You sound different.

Pip Do I?

Jo Suppose your teaching's having an effect. That's good. Biddy sends her love, by the way.

Pip Yes, I've been meaning to get in touch, but the course, it's, uh . . .

Jo Her great-aunt died.

Pip Oh, no.

Jo I sent you an invitation to the funeral, but I suppose you didn't get it.

Pip I've been busy.

Jo Luckily, Biddy wasn't exactly torn to bits about it. Her great-aunt wasn't the most horrible person I'd ever met, but she was in the running. Still, it's the sort of time you need friends around you.

Pip I'm sure she dealt with it okay. Good old Biddy.

Jo *gives* **Pip** *a disappointed look.*

Jo She's staying with me now. In your old room. She helps out with the rent, keeps the place tidy, helps me keep my head screwed on.

Pip That's good. I'm glad to hear that.

Jo It's been nice, because . . . well, I'm so happy for you, Philip, I am. But I do miss you, ever so slightly. Every now and again.

Pip Why are you calling me Philip, Mum?

Jo I can hardly keep calling you Pip, look at you now.

Pip I'd much prefer it if you did.

Jo No, it wouldn't be right. You're a proper grown man now, with your studies and your city life. I wouldn't feel right calling you Pip.

Pip   If that's what you want.

How's uh . . . how's Orlick?

Jo   Sacked. Fell into the bottle, saw it coming a mile off. Got too rough with people.

Pip   Rough with suspects?

Jo   Suspects, witnesses, the guv, you name it. He had it coming. Haven't seen him in weeks.

Pip   Can't say I'm not happy about it.

Jo   No, you two never did get on, did you. You'd never have known it to hear him. Just after you left town, he couldn't stop singing your praises, telling everyone who'd listen that he'd taught you everything you knew, that he'd always known you'd go far.

Pip   He didn't raise me, you did.

Jo   I did what I could.

Pip   You did everything!

Jo   Please don't judge him, Philip. He may have made a complete pig's ear of his life, but he's still a human being, same as you or me. There but for the grace of God, right?

Pip   Yes. Yes, of course.

A long, awkward pause.

Can I . . . would you like a cup of tea?

Jo   No, I'd better get moving.

Pip   But you've only just got here.

Jo   I came to see how you were doing, and it looks like you're living well and working hard, so I'll leave you to it. Besides, I was hoping to fit Tussaud's in before the train.

Pip   I could come with you.

Jo That's alright, Philip. I wasn't even going to come and bother you at all, but Biddy insisted, she said I should.

Pip Well, she was right.

Jo Maybe she was.

Jo *gives* **Pip** *a kiss on the cheek and hugs him.* **Pip** *is deeply troubled by how awkward this has all been.*

Pip Well . . . thanks so much for coming. I'll be in touch soon, promise.

Jo *looks at* **Pip** *with love, a pained smile of acceptance on her face.*

Jo That'd be nice.

Jo *turns and leaves.*

Pip *watches her go, then paces. He goes back to the desk, tries to get back to work, but is too distracted. He knows something has changed between him and* **Jo**, *but he can't work out what. His reverie is broken by* **Herbert**, *who bursts into the room.*

Herbert Billy! Thank God you're here! It's two-for-one cocktails at Joe Allen's!

Pip No!

Herbert Suit yourself.

Herbert *launches himself back out the door.* **Pip** *continues to work, in a frenzy, typing, flinging books open, cross-referencing, scribbling notes, tying himself in knots. Finally, he slams the books shut and collapses onto the desk, panting.*

Jaggers *enters, holding a rolled-up diploma. He slaps it onto the desk in front of* **Pip**, *who grabs it and holds it aloft in triumph.* **Jaggers** *then slams another enormous book onto the table.* **Pip** *groans and stands up. He picks up the book and begins leafing through it, walking around to the other side of the table.*

Jaggers *circles the table and sits down where* **Pip** *was, taking them through to the next scene.*

Twenty-one

Jaggers' office, nearly four years into Pip's time at LSE. Pip, now 25, sets the book down on the desk in front of Jaggers, now 49.

Jaggers   Once the results of your LPC are in, we shall discuss your placement. If you've passed, that is.

Pip   My placement! It feels like I just got here.

Jaggers   Have you thought about which firm you'd like to spend the year with? I understand our old colleague, Bentley Drummle, is doing very well in private practice. Perhaps you could give him a call?

Pip   I'll . . . give it some serious thought.

Jaggers   Speaking of Drummle, have you seen much of Estella since she came to town?

The mention of Drummle and Estella's names in the same sentence gives Pip a chill.

Pip   No, Mister Jaggers, not for a few months now.

Jaggers   Pity. Her opening at the Reservoir was quite something. Didn't understand what any of it was supposed to mean, of course, but the shapes were nice. I never imagined someone so cold and aloof could produce anything so sensual, so tactile.

Pip   I was sent an invitation, Mister Jaggers, but I thought better of going.

Jaggers   Hm. There was another matter I wanted to discuss with you.

Pip   If it relates to Estella or Drummle, or, worse, both of them, then please, Mister Jaggers, spare me.

Jaggers   No, not at all, Mister Pirrip, it's about your flatmate.

Pip   Herbert?

Jaggers   Yes, Mister Pocket. Has he discussed his money troubles with you?

Pip   I didn't know he had any.

Jaggers   Flat broke, to speak frankly.

Pip   I had no idea . . . I never would have thought, the way he's been living.

Jaggers   I fear you may have identified the problem. And, given that you yourself have been drawing very freely from an almost unlimited well of funds – perhaps the idea of money running out seems rather alien to you now.

Pip   Perhaps. Poor Herbert. He's always talking about going into practice.

Jaggers   Talk is one thing. If he carries on like this, it will certainly never happen. His work is appreciated at the school, but there is a glass ceiling to the role of Research Fellow, both in responsibility and in potential, and Mister Pocket has been butting his head up against this very ceiling for some years now.

Pip   If he'd only held a little back.

Jaggers   Unlikely, Mister Pirrip. To speak frankly, I think he's scared.

Pip   Scared of failure?

Jaggers   Scared of success. To incapacitate yourself to the point of inevitable failure is comforting, in a way. To gamble, and risk winning something worth living up to, is a far more frightening prospect. Anyway, if you think you might be able to caution Herbert with a bit of friendly advice at some point, I suspect he'd listen to you.

Pip   Mister Jaggers, I have a question.

Jaggers   If it relates to the identity of your benefactor, I must ask you to cast your mind back to the stipulations I laid out for you in the Blue Boar.

Pip   No, it's not that, but it's about that person, and their stipulations.

Jaggers   Go on.

Pip   They've given me complete control over this allowance, correct?

Jaggers   That is correct.

Pip   And they've put you in charge of the distribution, yes?

Jaggers   They have indeed.

Pip   In that case, I want to make some changes to the distribution.

Jaggers   I hope you're not thinking what I think you're thinking.

Pip   I want half of the monthly transfer to be forwarded to Mister Herbert Pocket, starting immediately. And, with the first payment, enough money from my savings to fund his speedy exit from this department into a private office of his choosing, plus the price of an engraved brass plaque.

Jaggers   Mister Pirrip, permit me to run over on my fingers the major bridges of the City of London.

Jaggers *counts the bridges off his fingers as he speaks.*

Of course there are London, Tower, Vauxhall, Westminster and Waterloo bridges. But there are also Hungerford, Blackfriars, Millennium, Southwark and Lambeth. Now that the cursed garden bridge has had a stake driven through its heart, that's ten.

Pip   I don't understand you.

Jaggers   Choose your bridge, Mister Pirrip, and take a walk upon it. Throw your money from the highest point of the bridge of your choosing and you will know the end of it. Give money to a friend and you'll know an end of it too, of course, but it will be a less pleasant and profitable end.

Pip This is very discouraging.

Jaggers It's meant to be.

Pip Nonetheless, as the inheritor of this legacy, I am not asking, I am insisting. Or else I'll have to go to my own bank and have them set up a standing order through a proxy account. Do you really want me to leave such a significant amount of money in the care of a high street banker?

Jaggers Hm.

Pip I would very much appreciate it if you would arrange this for me, Mister Jaggers, and if you could let Herbert know about his good luck. However, tell him the money is his on two conditions. Firstly, that he must use this money to set himself up as a solicitor as soon as possible. Secondly, that he must –

Jaggers – must never know the identity of his benefactor, thank you, Mister Pirrip, I know the script by now. You know, I hoped that when I gave up private practice, I would also give up watching people fritter their money away.

Pip Frittered for a good cause, at least.

Jaggers Good causes are not my stock in trade.

Pip You've looked after me well enough.

Jaggers That was different.

Pip How so?

Jaggers In your case . . . but oh, no, no. I'll let you squander your generous allowance however you please, Mister Pirrip, but you can't twist me around. I invented twisting. I am the arch twister. If you think you're going to fool me into revealing anything about the source of the money, you've got another think coming. Now get out of my office. I have a considerable amount of money to flush down the toilet.

Pip Good afternoon, Mister Jaggers.

Pip *exits the office.*

Twenty-two

Herbert's *flat, the same afternoon.* **Herbert**, *now 29, runs into the living room, hearing someone coming through the door. He is frantic, wild-eyed.*

Herbert   Billy? Billy, is that you?

Pip   Who else would it be?

Herbert   Billy, the . . . the money! The money, Billy!

Pip   What money?

Herbert   I didn't have any money! No money, you understand? Kaput! Gone!

Pip   Herbert, you should have said something.

Herbert   Ah, ah, ah, no, but now, you see . . . money EVERYWHERE!

Pip   Slow down! How? What happened? Who gave you the money?

Herbert   I don't know. All I know is I need to get to Jaggers' office pronto to discuss brass plaques and getting listed on Yell.

Herbert *hurriedly puts on his shoes and a coat.*

Pip   Who could have done it? Your family, maybe?

Herbert   Ha! No.

Pip   Or Miss Havisham?

Herbert   No, with my surname, she'd never even give me a cold. God, I wish I knew!

Pip   Take it from me, Herbert. Leave it. Just don't blow this now.

Herbert *realises who he's talking to.*

Herbert   Of course. Of course. Forget it for the moment, then. Billy?

Pip   Yes, Herbert?

Herbert *flings his arms around* **Pip** *and hugs him tight.*

Herbert   I'm terrified.

Pip   It'll pass.

Herbert *sprints out the door.* **Pip** *watches him go, beaming.*

There is a knock at the door.

Pip   Hello?

Enter **Magwycz**, *now 62, dressed shabbily, bowed and shivering.*

Magwycz   Mister Pip?

Pip   Excuse me, who are you?

Magwycz   You are Mister Pip?

Pip   How do you know my name?

Magwycz   Is on your doorbell.

Pip   Right. Yes. I'm him. Can I help you?

Magwycz   Yes. Yes, it is you. You can give me just one minute? Is cold outside, I travel long way, my legs are tired.

Pip   Uh, yes. I suppose so. Have a seat. But I can't let you stay long, I need to . . .

Magwycz   Pimlico, very nice.

Pip   Thank you, uh, we like it.

Magwycz   A place for a real gentleman.

Pip   I don't know about that.

Magwycz   Oh, you are real gentleman, Mister Pip. Look at you. Grown into a real gentleman, you make good life for yourself. Nice place with books for clever people. Good friends, and a future, I am right?

Pip   Look, excuse me, but . . . if you don't tell me what you want, I'll have to ask you to leave.

Magwycz   You don't remember.

Pip   Remember? Do I know you?

Magwycz *stands, goes over to* **Pip**. **Pip** *holds his ground, nervously.*

Magwycz   You remember the young man. You lock your door, you hide under your sheets, but this young man he get to you, and he tear you open.

Pip   But . . . oh my God.

Magwycz   Yes. Yes, you remember him.

Pip   What . . . what are you doing here?

Magwycz   I come to see if my investment come to good ends. I see that it does.

Pip   Your . . . investment?

Magwycz   You must wonder, Mister Pip, all these years, who make sure of your good fortune.

Pip *realises the truth.*

Pip   But . . . no.

Magwycz   You're welcome.

Pip   But I don't . . . I never even knew your name.

Magwycz   Abel Magwycz. Condemned man. Fugitive. Hired killer.

Pip   Killer? Wait, what are you doing here? You want your money? Or some kind of payback, maybe? What is this?

Magwycz   Listen to me, my boy! You don't listen! I tell you, I want only to see you made good. If you know how it feel to see your gentleman's apartment, your gentleman's clothes, your gentleman's life. You know, you are only person who ever show me kindness, even for a moment? I do bad things in my life, real bad. And at worst, at coldest, at darkest, I see your face. And I send you everything I got. Everything I make from bad life, I give you. And here you are.

Pip   I . . . I don't know what to . . .

There is a 'clunk' from outside. **Magwycz** *reacts as if it were a gunshot.*

Magwycz   What was that? You expect someone?

Pip *runs off in the direction of the sound.*

Pip   Hello? Who's that? Excuse me?

Offstage, running footsteps can be heard.

I didn't see . . . they were too quick. They're gone.

Magwycz   I know who is. I didn't think he find me so soon.

Pip   Who?

Magwycz   Compeyson. When I was with Brentford Security Company. Fancy name for killers. We get paid, we get paid good. We kill, we capture, we take over. For militia, Americans, British, don't matter. If they pay, we fight. They find me young, take me from my home where I got nothing, they tell me I make good money and they teach me to kill.

Pip *runs over and looks out the window, trying not to be spotted from the street.*

Magwycz   Me, I got no choice. Nothing for me back home, no money, no job, no hope. But Compeyson, different case completely. Gentleman. British Army, officer, world at his feet. He go private because he make more money from dirty killing jobs. We go on one job, government stuff in South America. Job is take out one militia to make way for different militia. Easy money. But Compeyson, he still want more.

Pip *goes back to the door and looks out into the hallway.*

Pip   No sign of anyone. Compeyson, he's after you?

Magwycz   Probable. We got beef.

Pip   Wait. He was the other man? The one you caught . . . after we first met?

Magwycz   Yes. His fault we get stuck on South America job. He tells the other side how we get in, and when, and where. For quick payoff. Joke on him. They do the double-cross on Compeyson. No need keep him alive, not if they found us already, so no money, just ten thousand bullets with his name on. But he miss them all.

This is all beginning to sink in. **Pip** *is horrified.*

Pip   No, no, this isn't right.

Magwycz   We separated, but I know his route home. We got same bad friends.

Pip   It wasn't supposed to be . . . this.

Magwycz   I follow him, all the way to ferry from Calais, but we get caught at Folkestone. In police van, I ask him, 'your plan work real good, you think?' He don't say anything, don't even look at me, so I get mad, I go for him. Police jump on us, we fight. Van crashes. Compeyson, he get away from me. I swear, never again. He never get away again. This, this when I meet you.

Pip   So this . . . this is all because . . . I just happened to be there?

Magwycz   You just happen to save my life.

Beat as **Pip** *tries to process all this.*

Pip   So you escaped again? After my mother arrested you.

Magwycz   They wanted to send us back to South America, back to death. But last minute, just before plane, Compeyson slip away again, and no way I go to firing squad without him, so I got to break out and go too.

Pip Did you kill anyone? Gun down a few coppers on your way out?

Magwycz No, no. Though maybe a couple not walk the same no more.

Pip Oh, God.

Magwycz Compeyson escapes me. No revenge for Magwycz and nowhere to go. I get new name – Provis, Mister Provis I was. Companies need people like me. Security Consultant. Too old to fight, but I teach bad bastards how to get worse and they pay me good. I tell myself, maybe I never get Compeyson, but you, Mister Pip. I always got you.

Pip Wonderful.

Magwycz This, Mister Pip, this is what keeps me alive! Anybody looks down on me with judgement, police, soldier, whatever, I think to myself, 'back in England is gentleman twice as noble as you! And he is my gentleman.'

Pip And this is where it all came from? This flat, this life, all this money? From killing.

Magwycz Pass your judgement on me if you like, it don't bother me. Judge my life, my actions, go ahead, I got it coming. But at least I know I done good by you.

Pip So it's . . . payment for services rendered? A reward? A bribe? What?

Magwycz Is money. Money is money, don't matter where it came from, only matters where it goes. The only way you can make change in this world, money.

Pip It could have been anyone. Anyone there that night. Couldn't it?

Magwycz Could be. Who cares? You were there.

Pip No rhyme or reason. No . . . destiny, no plan. Just money.

Magwycz   Just money.

Pip   Why did you come back?

Magwycz   Aah, Provis don't live so long. People find out about Magwycz, Interpol still want my guts, so I run. Nobody in security hires wanted men. Don't worry, Mister Pip, my boy, still plenty of money left for you. Jaggers hides it good.

Pip   No, that's . . . that's not what I was thinking about.

Magwycz   Compeyson. I know is Compeyson rat me out.

Herbert *comes in,* **Pip** *jumps,* **Magwycz** *hardly moves, but tenses up, ready to pounce.*

Herbert   It's all sorted, Billy! Jaggers is sending . . .

Herbert *sees* **Magwycz.**

Herbert   Oh. Hello. I didn't realise we had . . . company.

Magwycz   Your friend?

Pip   Yes, please don't kill him. Herbert, did you see anybody out there?

Herbert   Out where?

Pip   In the street? In the hallway? Anybody hanging around?

Herbert   No, nobody.

Magwycz   Good. He don't know I'm here for sure. If he do, he already kill you both, then me.

Herbert *and* **Pip** *look at each other.*

Herbert   Aren't you going to introduce us?

Pip   Herbert Pocket, meet Abel Magwycz. My generous benefactor.

Herbert   Good Lord. Uh, pleasure to make your acquaintance.

Magwycz   Likewise.

Pip   Listen. What can I do? What do you want? Revenge?

Magwycz   No, no. I get old. Tired. I don't need nothing no more, I just want rest. I want to go home. But Compeyson, he looking for me. He got score to settle with me too, now. He would run free, if I didn't stop him back then.

Jaggers, Jaggers is only man in the world I can trust. Long time ago, Provis days, we was good friends. I get him evidence, I find people, and in exchange, he keep wolf from my door in Britain. But nobody can help Magwycz. Too much dirt on Magwycz. Especially if Compeyson find me. He knows where I bury my bodies.

Herbert   Wait . . . Compeyson?

Pip *and* **Magwycz** *turn to* **Herbert**.

Magwycz   You know him?

Herbert   No, but . . . well, all I know is . . . Compeyson was the name of Miss Havisham's lover. The one who left her at the altar.

Pause.

Magwycz   You don't need this, I know. I can leave. I can leave right now, out the door, if you want. But please, Mister Pip, whatever I done, do not refuse my money, do not refuse this life. If you do that, you take away the only good thing I ever did.

Pip *thinks, then puts his hand on* **Magwycz's** *shoulder.*

Pip   You take my room. Don't go out, don't answer the door, don't even go near the windows. Stay in there and keep the door shut.

Magwycz *beams, embraces* **Pip**.

Magwycz   Thank you, my boy. If you knew how it feel to see you now.

Magwycz *slouches off to* **Pip**'s *bedroom.*

Herbert *looks at* **Pip**, *aghast.* **Pip** *looks back to him.*

Pip   And how was your evening?

Pip *and* **Herbert** *grab their coats, fast forwarding to the next morning.*

Twenty-three

Pip *and* **Herbert** *walk out into the cold morning outside* **Herbert**'s *flat, the next day.*

Pip   Where's it moored?

Herbert   Over in Haggerston, it's just a little houseboat, my uncle never uses it. I can move him there this morning.

Pip   In daylight?

Herbert   We'll get lost among the commuters.

Pip   Yes. Good. Talk to Jaggers first. Tell him I know everything.

Herbert   Goody. A morning of carefully-phrased euphemisms for 'escorting a wanted criminal out of the country'.

Pip   Well don't tell the whole world about it.

Herbert   Sorry. Where are you going?

Pip   Home.

Herbert   At a time like this?

Pip   It can't wait. I'll be back tonight.

Herbert   If you're sure.

Estella, *now 25, appears in the street.*

Estella   Pip?

Pip   Estella?

Herbert   I'd . . . better go find Jaggers.

Herbert *nods to* **Estella** *and hurries away.*

Pip   Estella, what are you doing here? It's six in the morning.

Estella   I needed to be sure I'd catch you.

Pip   This isn't the best time.

Estella   I'm leaving town today.

Pip   Where are you going?

Estella   Back to Berlin. My exhibition's transferring.

Pip   Well, good luck with it, but –

Estella   Bentley's coming with me.

Pip *sighs.*

Pip   I thought he might.

Estella   We're going to be married.

Pip *looks at* **Estella**.

Pip   Why are you here? Why did you come here to tell me this?

Estella   I wanted you to hear it from me.

Pip   Because you wanted my opinion? You can have it. You're making a mistake.

Estella   You might think so.

Pip   I do think so. And it hurts me to see you make it. I can't bear to think of people talking about you, saying 'she married the most vain, obnoxious man in London'.

Estella   I can bear it.

Pip   Why are you doing this? You can't love him.

Estella   No, I can't love him, or anybody! I've told you so, and still you don't believe me.

Pip   I don't care if you never think of me again as long as you live, but at least try to find someone better than Drummle! Miss Havisham isn't in charge of you any more!

Estella   Who said anything about Miss Havisham? This is my decision.

Pip   Your decision, to throw your life away for a man like that?

Estella   Yes. My decision. I've grown tired of the life I've led these last few years. It has very few charms left for me, so why shouldn't I throw it away? Don't be afraid that I'll be a blessing to Bentley, I sincerely doubt I'll be that. Do we have to part on this note, Pip? Is this how we're going to say goodbye?

Pip   I wish you'd never told me. I wish you'd just gone and never said a word. I could have lived with that much more easily.

Estella   Don't be ridiculous. You'll have forgotten all about me in a week or two.

Pip   Forget you? You're everything. You're the pavement under my feet. You're the roof over my head. Every thought I've had since the day we met has been whispered in your voice. You created me. And now I have to watch you run into the arms of a preening nobody, and not . . .

Estella   . . . Not you?

Pip   Not me.

Estella   So you want me to deceive you? To entrap you?

Pip   Do you deceive and entrap him?

Estella   Yes! Him and many others! All of them! All of them except you!

Pause.

I have to go.

Estella *leaves.* **Pip** *watches her go until she is out of sight, and then turns and marches away in the other direction.*

Twenty-four

Satis House, that afternoon. **Miss Havisham,** *now 61, sits by her great dining table, looking older and more frail than ever.*

Pip *walks in and stands respectfully aside, waiting to be called in.*

Miss Havisham *notices him.*

Miss Havisham . . . Pip? Is it real?

Pip It's me, Miss Havisham.

Miss Havisham *strains to see him.*

Miss Havisham Come closer, boy, let me look at you.

Pip *does as he's told.*

Miss Havisham No, not a boy any more. A man. A gentleman, no less. Very good. You have come from London, I suppose?

Pip Yes, Miss Havisham.

Miss Havisham Have you seen Estella?

Pip Just this morning, Miss Havisham.

Miss Havisham Then you have heard the happy news?

Pip I've heard the news, anyway.

Miss Havisham Ah. You still love her, don't you.

Pip It wouldn't be right to say so, not about a woman who's engaged to be married.

Miss Havisham *reaches out and grabs* **Pip**'*s arm.*

Miss Havisham   Love her, love her, love her! How does she use you?

Pip   She doesn't use me, Miss Havisham.

Miss Havisham   I adopted her to be loved, Pip. I bred her and educated her to be loved. I developed her into what she is, that she might be loved.

Pip   But you never did the same for me, did you?

Miss Havisham *is struck slightly dumb by this. She glares at* **Pip**, *inscrutably.*

Pip   I wanted to believe you had. And I think you liked me believing it. It fed the dream of Estella which you'd planted in my head. But you never had any hand in my expectations, nor any interest in them, except that it might keep me close to your daughter.

Miss Havisham   My adopted daughter.

Pip   When Compeyson left, I don't imagine he had any idea what he'd left with you. And maybe, standing in that wedding dress that day, you didn't either.

Miss Havisham   What.

Pip   Or perhaps you did, but you knew you could get away without telling anybody until after the wedding.

Miss Havisham   No, no!

Pip   As if the shame of being left in favour of profit weren't bad enough, to be left alone, holding the baby, would have been unbearable for a woman of your standing.

Miss Havisham   Shut up! Lies!

Pip   Much more noble to take in a poor abandoned child out of kindness. And a blank slate for you to write your revenge on, with no idea who she is or where she came from. The details of her sudden appearance could easily be whitewashed with a bit of money. I've learned a lot about what can be achieved with money, Miss Havisham.

Miss Havisham *has broken down into tears.*

Miss Havisham   What have I done. What have I done.

Pip *puts a hand on her shoulder.*

Pip   I need something from you. I have recently set a
friend of mine up in business as a solicitor. The expense is
more than I can cover. I would very much appreciate it if
you could cover the rest.

Miss Havisham   Is this blackmail?

Pip   No. Nothing could be gained from telling anyone.
Nothing except causing Estella a great deal of pain, and I
want that less than anything else in the world.

Miss Havisham   You do love her. Love is blind devotion.
Unquestioning self-humiliation. Utter submission. Trust and
belief against yourself and against the whole world. Giving
up your whole heart and soul to the smiter – as I did.

Pip   Yes. Yes, Miss Havisham, I do love her.

Miss Havisham *breaks down, claws at* **Pip**'s *clothes, weeps into
his arm.*

Miss Havisham   What have I done? All I wanted was to save
her from misery like mine! At first, I wanted nothing more!

Pip   I hope so, Miss Havisham.

Miss Havisham   But as she grew up, and promised to be
very beautiful, I became greedy. With my praises and my
jewels and my teachings, and with my own unhappy self
always nearby as a warning to back and point my lessons, I
stole her heart away and put ice in its place!

Pip   Better to have left her a real heart, even to be bruised
or broken.

Miss Havisham *sobs, gasps, composes herself.*

Miss Havisham   Will Jaggers manage the transaction? For
your friend?

Pip   Yes, Jaggers will take care of it.

Miss Havisham *takes a pencil and paper from the table and scribbles an instruction, then signs it. She hands it to* **Pip**.

Miss Havisham   And if you can ever bear it, take the pencil and write there, under my name, 'I forgive her'. Even if it isn't until long after my broken heart is dust.

Pip   I have nothing to forgive you for, Miss Havisham. I would have loved Estella whatever the case. Whenever I met her, under whatever circumstance, I would have loved her.

Miss Havisham *nods and exits.*

Pip *surveys the paper and, satisfied, folds it up and puts it in his pocket.*

Pip *walks out of the front doors of Satis House into the afternoon sun. He turns to take one last look up at Satis House, but is shocked by what he sees.*

Pip   Miss Havisham? MISS HAVISHAM, NO!

Pip *sees* **Miss Havisham** *leap from the top of Satis House and sprints to catch her.*

Ambulance sirens, police radio chatter.

Twenty-five

Pip *sits outside Satis House, his arm in a sling. Sirens fade down.*

Biddy *enters.*

Biddy   The medics say if you hadn't been there to break her fall, she'd be dead for sure.

Pip   Is she going to be alright?

Biddy   They don't know. She was barely conscious.

Pip   Did she say anything?

Biddy She wasn't making any sense. She just kept saying 'write under my name', over and over again.

Pip Mm.

Biddy You did a good thing, Pip.

Pip Did I?

Biddy Well, you tried anyway.

Biddy *sits beside* **Pip** *and puts her head on his shoulder.*

Pip Good to see you too.

Enter **Jo***, now 44.*

Jo They're taking her to the hospital for observation, but she's completely unconscious. Ambulance boys say all we can do is wait and see. Oh, Pip.

Jo *comes over and strokes* **Pip**'s *hair, doting mother again for a moment.*

Jo Oh, my poor little Pip.

Pip *looks up at his mother, delighted to hear her call him that again.*

Pip Can you give me a lift to the station?

Jo No. You're not travelling, not today, not with your arm knackered six ways over. I'm going with the ambulance. You can go back to the flat and get a decent meal and a good night's sleep in. Then you can go home.

Jo *exits towards the ambulance.*

Pip Feels like I'm home already.

Biddy Still got keys?

Pip You not coming?

Biddy Need to explain to the headmaster why I ran out in the middle of a lesson.

Pip Thanks, Biddy.

Biddy I was worried. The old lady nearly finished you off.

Pip   Take more than that.

Biddy   Don't get too full of yourself or I'll twist your arm.

Pip   Alright, I'm going.

Pip *and* **Biddy** *exit in opposite directions.*

Twenty-six

Jo's *flat.* **Pip** *walks through the front door.*

He takes a second to look at the old place. He takes a deep breath in through his nose, taking in all the old smells.

Suddenly, **Orlick,** *now 31, comes barrelling through the door after him, a half-drunk bottle of whiskey in his hand. He is dressed as if he has been sleeping rough for several days. He grabs* **Pip**'s *broken arm and twists it around behind his back.* **Pip** *screams in agony.*

Orlick   Now I've got you.

Pip   Who's that?!

Orlick   All in good time.

Orlick *shoves* **Pip** *over to the kitchen table and seats him, releasing his arm.* **Pip** *pants and gasps in pain, clumsily replacing the sling. He looks up at his assailant.*

Pip   Jesus Christ. Orlick. What is this?

Orlick   Not so big and important now. Golden boy.

Pip   Orlick, whatever you think you're doing, it's a mistake!

Orlick   Mistake!? You ruined me.

Pip   That's not the way I hear it.

Orlick   Shut up!

Orlick *slaps* **Pip** *in the face, swigs from the whiskey bottle.*

Orlick   You've been in old Orlick's way ever since you was a kid.

Pip   I don't know what you mean, Orlick, I never wanted to hurt you!

Orlick   Not enough you poison my name to your mother, my friend, a woman I could have loved!

Pip   Orlick, please.

Orlick   But you have to turn Biddy against me as well, the sweetest, kindest girl I ever knew.

Pip   Biddy didn't want you, Orlick, I had nothing to do with it!

Orlick   I am TALKING!

Orlick *punches* **Pip** *in the stomach.*

Orlick   I could have done something with my life, if I'd had the luck you had! If it had been as easy for me as it was for you, you think I'd be here now? But everything that was ever due to Orlick went to Mister Pip instead, and he never appreciated it, none of it. But I got you now, you little rat. I went looking for Mister Pip in his fancy London digs and what did I find? Abel Magwycz, hired killer, stopping in on his little pet city gent.

Pip   Jesus, it was you.

Orlick   I could destroy you. I could turn you and your Uncle Magwycz in with all your dirty money and leave you to rot in a cell for aiding and abetting a dangerous fugitive.

Orlick *takes an enormous swig from the bottle.*

But I'd rather have your life.

Pip *doesn't dare to move, but tries to conceal his terror.*

Pip   That's it, is it? You're going to kill me because I was lucky? Because a couple of women turned you down? What happened to you?

Orlick   You happened to me, Mister Pip. And now you're going to pay for it.

Orlick *swigs.*

Pip   Can you do it, Orlick? Kill an injured man, one you've known since he was a child? Are you prepared to do that?

Orlick *considers the amount of liquid left in the bottle.*

Orlick   Almost.

Orlick *drains the bottle and turns it around in his hands, ready to use it as a club. He feels the heft of it in his hand, then turns to* **Pip**.

Orlick   If you was of a mind to scream, now would be the time.

Pip   HELP! SOMEONE! HELP ME!

Suddenly **Jo**, **Biddy** *and* **Herbert** *burst in and leap at* **Orlick**. **Orlick** *struggles, swings at them drunkenly, but is too far gone to land a hit.* **Biddy** *and* **Herbert** *scrabble at his arms and legs, holding him back.*

Jo   Stand down, officer!

Jo *hits* **Orlick** *in the face with everything she's got.* **Orlick** *recoils, looks like he's about to rally, then hits the deck, out cold.* **Biddy** *runs to* **Pip**'s *side, where* **Pip** *is keening from the twist to his arm.* **Jo** *rolls* **Orlick** *over and slaps the cuffs on him.*

Biddy   Pip, did he hurt you?

Biddy *inspects* **Pip**'s *arm and his sling.* **Pip** *hisses in pain at her touch.*

Pip   Very nearly. What the bloody hell are you doing here?

Herbert   Magwycz told me he saw somebody shadowing you when you left the flat.

Pip   I told him not to go near the windows!

Jo *talks into her radio.*

Jo   Dispatch, this is six-one, suspect apprehended. Request backup, he's a heavy one.

Jo *goes out to the hallway.* **Herbert** *looks down at the felled* **Orlick**.

Herbert   Did we do that?

Biddy   Mostly Jo, but we can call it a team effort if it makes you happy.

Pip   Herbert. Did you get him to the canal?

Herbert   Yes, soon as I got back from Jaggers' office.

Pip   We have to get back to town.

Biddy   Are you kidding?

Pip   Herbert, we can't stay here. Orlick knows everything, by the time he wakes up, it might be too late.

Biddy   But your arm!

Pip   It'll keep for a couple of hours. We have to do it now!

Herbert   You're right.

Biddy   Do what, for Christ's sake?

Pip   I hope you never find out. Wish me luck.

Pip *storms out of the flat, cradling his arm.*

Herbert *starts after him, looks back and waves awkwardly to* **Biddy**.

Herbert   It was . . . nice to meet you.

Biddy   Go!

Herbert *hurries after* **Pip**. **Biddy** *looks down at* **Orlick**'*s unconscious body. Contemplates it for a moment, then gives it a sharp kick.*

Jo *reappears. She and* **Biddy** *drag away the still-unconscious* **Orlick** *between scenes.*

Twenty-seven

The canalside near Haggerston, late that night. The sound of lapping water, nearby traffic.

Pip *leads* **Magwycz** *from the boat onto the bank.* **Magwycz** *has been cleaned up, he wears a suit and tie and a smart overcoat.*

Magwycz   Your friend is on his way?

Pip   Finding us a car. Black cab should be anonymous enough.

Magwycz   Yes, thank you.

Pip   You just have to leave the talking to me. Try to look natural, like you're just any ordinary man taking a trip.

Magwycz   Ordinary, yes.

Pip   Herbert's got your new passport, it'll get you home. From there you'll be on your own.

Magwycz   Get me home is all I ask.

Magwycz *embraces* **Pip**. **Pip** *is surprised.*

Magwycz   Thank you, my boy. Thank you. If you know how it feel, to think you do this for me. If you know how it feel to walk free, and stand next to my boy after running so long.

Pip   I think I know freedom well enough.

Magwycz   Not until you lose it. Until you sit between four walls, you don't know what it is to be outside of them.

Pip   No. No, I suppose not.

Magwycz   But I hope you never know.

Suddenly two police officers appear, shining torches at **Pip** *and* **Magwycz**.

Police 1   Stop right there!

Pip   No!

Police 2   Abel Magwycz, I'm going to have to ask you to come with us.

Magwycz   I come quiet, but you leave this boy! He don't know who I am!

Pip   What are you doing?

Magwycz   I threaten his life! I tell him I kill him if he don't help me!

Police 1   We're not interested in this man, sir, we just want to ask you a few questions.

Magwycz   Questions! Ha! How you find me?

Compeyson *appears, unbound, dressed smartly.*

Compeyson   That's the man, officers.

Magwycz   Compeyson!

Compeyson   I'd know that face anywhere.

Magwycz   Never again!

Magwycz *leaps at the police officers, throws them to the ground, and grabs* **Compeyson**. *He beats him savagely, like a wild animal.* **Pip** *stands back and watches, horrified.*

Pip   Stop! Please!

Compeyson *fights back, to no avail.* **Magwycz** *throws him down on his front and beats his head on the stone path again and again, until he stops twitching.* **Compeyson** *is dead.*

Magwycz   Never again.

The police officers get back to their feet, dazed, see what has happened and raise their torches. They set upon **Magwycz**, *beating him into submission. As they attack,* **Magwycz** *laughs.*

Pip   No!

Pip *watches, helpless, as the police subdue* **Magwycz**. *When they have finished, they lay him out on the table, which becomes a hospital bed. They take* **Compeyson**'s *body away.*

Pip *lays a blanket over* **Magwycz**.

Twenty-eight

Pip *sits next to the half-alive* **Magwycz** *in the hospital, in the early morning, many days later.* **Pip**'s *arm is still in a sling.* **Magwycz** *lies still for a moment, then stirs, gently.*

Magwycz   Pip? My boy?

Pip   I'm here.

Magwycz   Good boy. Staying by your Uncle Magwycz.

Pip   I won't leave your side. Until they drag me away, I'll be as good to you as you were to me.

Magwycz   They drag you away soon. They send me to die.

Pip   The trial was a farce.

Magwycz   Sorry I missed it. Jaggers is good man, bet he put on a good show.

Pip   No mention of the arrest, no mention of you being beaten half to death.

Magwycz *laughs weakly.*

Magwycz   I was asking for it. I always been asking for it.

Pip   The British courts don't want to know anything about it. They want to send you to South America. In your state!

Magwycz   I taken my death sentence from God, I take theirs as well.

Pip   Don't say that.

Magwycz   You done everything for me, my boy.

Pip *takes* **Magwycz***'s hand.*

Pip   I couldn't even do one thing right for you.

Magwycz   You could turn me away, you heard all the bad I done in my life. But you don't. You stand by me, you do everything for me, even at my worst, always at my worst. Only good thing I know in my life – when I get lost in the dark, Pip is there. That is best of all.

Pip   Magwycz. Abel. Listen, please . . . I don't know how to say this, but . . . it isn't me. I'm not the man you wanted, I'm not . . . I'm not a good person.

Magwycz *chuckles, very weak now.*

Magwycz My boy. If you knew how it feel . . . to see . . .

Magwycz *tails off mid-sentence. He rattles out a last breath.* **Pip** *watches him slip away, teary-eyed.* **Pip** *gently lays* **Magwycz**'*s hand on his chest, then stands.*

Pip Nurse?

Pip, *shellshocked, steps out of* **Magwycz**'*s room, into the hallway.*

Pip Nurse?

Herbert *appears, gingerly approaches* **Pip**.

Herbert Not quite. Is he . . .?

Pip *nods.*

Herbert Ah. Escaped justice again.

Pip *smiles, sadly.*

Pip He'll be pleased with that.

Herbert I'm sorry, Billy.

Pip I wanted answers. I got them.

Herbert Yes. Oh, I brought this for you. Came in the post this morning.

Herbert *produces an envelope and hands it to* **Pip**. **Pip** *opens it, reads the contents and smiles.*

Pip What a day.

Herbert Yes?

Pip On top of everything else, I need to find a firm.

Herbert *is pleased, excited, but can't fully express it in the sombre mood.*

Herbert Really?

Pip   Got room for an apprentice at Pocket Solicitors next year?

Herbert   Oh! Oh, yes. Of course. I mean, I need to move into the office first, but – yes!

Pip   Thanks. Only seems right.

Herbert   Yes.

Pip   Need to make sure my investment pays off.

Herbert   Yes.

Herbert *stops, thinks. Looks at* **Pip**.

Herbert   You –

Herbert *stops. Thinks. Laughs, stops short. Throws his arms around* **Pip**.

Herbert   I knew it!

Pip   Ha.

Herbert   I mean, I didn't know, but I knew, I thought, I suspected. A bit.

Pip   Oh yes, yes, I'm sure you did.

Herbert *is overjoyed. He tries to retain his composure out of respect for* **Magwycz**.

Herbert   God bless you, Billy.

Pip   It's nothing.

Herbert   It's not nothing! It's the kindest thing anyone ever did for me!

Pip *hears echoes of* **Magwycz** *in* **Herbert**'s *words. He doesn't say anything.*

Herbert   Listen, I . . . I was thinking of taking a trip to your neck of the woods. Soon. Come with me. It'd do you good to see Jo, at a time like this.

Pip   And Biddy?

Herbert   Well. Yes. Biddy too. If you like.

Pip   That sounds nice.

Herbert *puts a hand on* **Pip***'s shoulder.*

Herbert   Billy. I know it's . . . but it'll be alright. You'll be alright.

Pip   I'll live.

Pip*'s 'I'll live' throws us far forward in time.*

Twenty-nine

Jo*'s flat, eleven years later.* **Pip***, now 36, his arm completely recovered, looks over the place. Older, he exudes far more confidence than we have seen from him before. He has settled into his life and wears it like a comfortable slipper. He calls to* **Jo***, who is offstage.*

Pip   I don't know why you insist on staying in this pokey little flat. I'm amazed it hasn't been condemned yet.

Jo*, now 55, shouts back from offstage.*

Jo   This is the home you were raised in, young man, and you will show it some respect! Sugar?

Pip   No thanks. Respect is one thing, but wouldn't you rather be a bit more comfortable?

Jo *arrives onstage, holding two cups of tea, which she places on the table.*

Jo   I get enough comfort at work.

Jo *spots a woodlouse on the table and smashes it with her fist.*
Got 'im.

Pip   You couldn't pound the cobbles all your life.

Jo   I don't know how you can live your whole life behind a desk, I've never been so bored.

Pip   I've got my hobbies. Whittling, the saxophone, you know.

Jo   How the other half lives. How is it at Pocket and Pirrip?

Pip   Temporarily out of action. Herbert and Biddy pulled out all the stops for their tenth, they're doing a little world tour.

Jo   Anything to get away from the office, I expect.

Pip   You expect just about right. So I'm at a loose end for a month or two.

Jo   Oh, Pip, what are you doing here?

Pip   Visiting my mother. That's allowed, isn't it?

Jo   But why aren't you off at some fashionable London hotspot, on a roof terrace somewhere, chatting up a nice girl? They exist, I've seen them.

Pip   Oh, I don't know. I've grown so used to being the third wheel. Old Uncle Pip. I'm perfectly happy turning into a withered old bachelor, thank you.

Jo *looks at* **Pip**.

Jo   It's still her, isn't it?

Pip   No. No, not at all.

Jo   Pip.

Pip   Well . . . I've never forgotten anybody who ever held a place in my heart, I suppose. But that dream is long dead, promise.

Jo   If you say so. Speaking of which, they're flogging off Miss Havisham's old place.

Pip   They finally settled the divorce, then?

Jo   See? You've been keeping tabs.

Pip   How did it come out?

Jo   Very well. For Drummle. Talk around town is that Satis House is all the poor girl managed to wrestle away from him. Perils of marrying a lawyer, I suppose. If you want to say goodbye to the place, you'd best do it today.

Pip   I'd better run, then.

Pip *gets up, kisses* **Jo**'s *cheek.*

Pip   I'll get you cosily retired one of these days.

Jo   Get lost, old man.

Jo *leaves.*

Thirty

Satis House, later that afternoon. **Pip** *surveys Satis House, totally immersed in his memories. He looks around at the house, long ago fallen to wrack and ruin.*

Pip   I didn't think this place could look more run down, but there you go.

Somehow it feels like I never left.

I can't remember how it felt to be a Pip who hadn't seen this place. A Pip who hadn't followed Estella down its long, dusty halls. Was it really Pip before, or was Pip born here, that day?

Estella, *now 36, appears, stepping gingerly towards* **Pip**.

Estella   Pip?

Pip *turns, not believing his eyes. He looks for a long time, wanting to be sure.*

Pip   Estella.

Estella   I've changed so much. It's a wonder you know me.

Pip Of course. You've come for one last visit?

Estella This land belongs to me. It's the only thing I've ever owned that I never gave up. Everything else has been taken from me, little by little. But I wouldn't let my home go. It's the only resistance I ever showed in all these wretched years.

Pip Are they going to build on the land?

Estella At last, yes. It hasn't been any use to anyone for a long time. But I wanted to see it again before it changes. Poor, poor old place.

Moment.

You're still in London?

Pip Yes. Still shackled to Herbert. You remember Herbert?

Estella You do well, I'm sure?

Pip I work pretty hard for a decent living, so yes, yes, I do well.

Estella I have often thought of you.

Pip *doesn't know how to respond.*

Estella Very often, of late. For a long time I tried to forget you, and what you gave me. One day I finally realised its importance, so since I couldn't honour it, I gave it a place in my heart.

Pip You've never lost your place in mine.

Pause.

Estella I didn't imagine I'd be able to say goodbye to you at the same time as this place. I'm glad.

Pip Is this goodbye?

Estella Certainly. You have your life in the city, and I have mine to rebuild. In the end, suffering was the greatest teacher I ever could have hoped for. Over the past few years,

I have been bent, and broken – but, I hope, into a better shape.

It has taught me to understand what your heart once was.

Be kind to me once more, Pip. Tell me we are friends.

Pip   Of course. Of course we're friends.

Estella   And shall continue friends apart?

Estella *looks at* **Pip**, *a note of genuine pleading in her eyes.*

Pip *walks close to her and takes her hand.* **Estella** *smiles. He looks deep into her eyes and speaks not to her, but to the audience.*

Pip   I took her hand in mine and we went out of the ruined place.

Pip *and* **Estella** *walk away from Satis House. They look at the landscape ahead of them.* **Pip** *continues to speak to the audience.*

Pip   The evening mists were rising now, and in all the broad expanse of tranquil light they showed to me, I saw no shadow of another parting from her.

Pip *and* **Estella** *turn and look at one another.*

The End.

For a complete listing of Bloomsbury
Methuen Drama titles, visit:

www.bloomsbury.com/drama

Follow us on Twitter and keep up to date
with our news and publications

@MethuenDrama